FOUNDATIONS OF WEALTH:

HOW TO BUILD A REAL ESTATE EMPIRE

WISDOM FROM THE BEST IN THE BUSINESS

FOUNDATIONS OF WEALTH:
HOW TO BUILD A REAL ESTATE EMPIRE

WISDOM FROM THE BEST IN THE BUSINESS

MARCEL ARSENAULT • JOHN HAMILTON
BEN LEEDS • GERALD MARCIL

Marcus & Millichap

Atlanta • Austin • Boise • Charlotte • Chicago • Cincinnati • Cleveland
Columbus • Dallas • Denver • Detroit • Encino • Ft. Lauderdale
Greenville • Houston • Indianapolis • Jacksonville • Las Vegas
Layfayette • Long Beach • Los Angeles • Madison • Manhattan
Miami • Milwaukee • Nashville • New Haven • Newport Beach
Oakland • Ontario • Orlando • Palo Alto • Philadelphia • Phoenix
Portland • Reno • Sacramento • Salt Lake City • San Antonio
San Diego • San Francisco • Seattle • Tampa • Washington, DC.

ISBN 0-9770733-0-0

This publication is designed to provide accurate and authoritative
information with regard to the subject matter but is sold with
the understanding that neither the authors nor the publishers are
engaged herein in rendering professional services.

To order copies:
Foundations of Wealth Publishing Company
2626 Hanover Street
Palo Alto, CA 94304
650-494-8900
or visit www.FoundationsOfWealth.com

First Edition
Printed in the United States of America

Contents

Profits from the sale of this book are being donated to charities chosen by each of the four experts whose experiences and ideas are presented here.

Acknowledgements

First and most importantly we would like to thank Marcel Arsenault, John Hamilton, Ben Leeds, and Gerald Marcil who invested their very valuable time and contributed their impressive success histories that are the foundation of this book. Their extensive interviews, numerous edits and valuable input increased our understanding of what it takes to be successful in the very challenging and competitive business of investing in income-producing real estate.

The four contributing investors were selected from our Hall of Fame nominees.

We offer a special thanks to Brian O'Connell who conducted the investor interviews and was instrumental in reducing to print the core of the narratives along with assisting in the editing of the balance of the book. We appreciate the counseling of Mahesh Grossman, who encouraged us to embark on this project. Marcus & Millichap Research Services and Hessam Nadji were significant contributors to the section dealing with the current and the future role of investment real estate in the United States economy.

Thanks to Al Pace of Pacific Property Company, Jim Kessler of Highland Development Company, Bill Powell of Meridian Property Company and Bob Miller of ERM Consultants for their help with the Annotations section.

Finally we would like to thank our nationwide network of brokers who participated in this project by nominating over one hundred and forty investors for the Marcus & Millichap Real Estate Investor Hall of Fame. The four contributing investors were selected from the Hall of Fame nominees.

George Marcus
Bill Millichap
Harvey Green

> *"Price is what you pay.*
> *Value is what you get."*
> *– Warren Buffet*

Warren Buffet has it right. The key to making money really *is* about what you get, not what you pay. That's especially true in the real estate world. Investors who see the market clearly and make decisions based on the best evidence available will go far in real estate.

The critical question: Could the founder take a vacation without the need to call or e-mail the office?

This book contains the real estate investment histories of four highly successful individuals. They describe the paths they took that resulted in the creation of four separate, self-sustaining, real estate empires—self-sustaining in that the companies they started would continue to flourish without the day-to-day input of the founder.

The critical question that we asked was, "If they so desired, could the founder take a vacation without

 ~ iii ~

the need to call or e-mail the office?" To fulfill such a qualification, the founder must have built a company consisting of a group of independent real estate entrepreneurs who are capable of managing and growing the business to the next level of success. The investors contributing to this book have achieved that goal and have also attained a level of financial security and freedom that gives them the option of pursuing other interests without the need to contact their offices "to see how things are going."

Since opening for business in 1971, the Marcus & Millichap Real Estate Investment Brokerage Company has faced the challenge of representing clients in the sale, purchase, exchange, and refinance of their investment real estate. From the perspective of an advisor/intermediary, our brokers have been active participants with a wide variety of investors, vendors, consultants, governmental agencies, brokers, and lending institutions in closing over $80 billion dollars of income-producing property in more than 20,000 transactions.

Our primary market segment has always been the principal-minded, individual investor. Although we have also represented institutional investors with multi-billion dollar portfolios, the majority of our transactions have been conducted on a face-to-face basis with the individual investor who is on the title. Within the private client segment, we have seen patterns of execution that have been repeated to the point where the roads to success can be identified— although those paths can still be hazardous. By following in the tracks of successful investors, we feel that many of the dangers can be avoided and that from a risk-adjusted basis, the probability of being able to build a substantial financial empire makes investment real estate a compelling asset opportunity.

Within our industry there are a considerable number of investors who have profited from the business of acquiring, improving, and actively managing their investment real estate. Within this population of successful individual investors, there exists a very limited number of real estate investor all-stars. This all-star segment has expanded the definition of success beyond that of individual practitioners managing limited income property portfolios.

Reducing to print the success histories of this breed of investor is challenging. They are typically consumed with their business and not particularly interested in the publication of their successes. We selected these superstar investors and asked their permission to present their stories and what they've learned for the benefit of other aspiring real estate investors. All four contributing investors also agreed to donate their share of any profits from the sale of this book to the charities of their choice.

We hope you find it informative and inspirational.

George Marcus
Bill Millichap
Harvey Green

Foundations of Wealth

Book Content & Reading Suggestions

T his book is divided into three sections.

✦ The investor success stories, which are the core of this book, are contained in Chapters 1 through 4.

✦ Chapter 5 outlines some of the basic concepts that influence the real estate market by product type, and offers some of our thoughts about the future of investment real estate.

✦ The final section—Annotations—is comprised of 65 detailed descriptions of strategies, pitfalls to avoid, professional tips, useful tools and resources, ideas, and concepts that expand and build on the investor commentaries.

This book can be read in several different sequences depending on your previous experience and your particular interest. However you use it, you will come away with a deeper understanding—both theoretical and practical—of how fortunes are made, and in some cases lost, in real estate investment:

1. Read the four success stories without referring to the annotations.

2. Read the success stories and refer to the referenced annotations in the order you encounter them.

3. Read all the annotations first, then the success stories.

Chapter 5, "A Growing Population," explains how demographics will drive real estate investment in the next 15 or so years; outlines the fundamentals that drive the investment real estate market; provides additional background about how the investment market is segmented; and how macro-economic trends influence the cyclical nature of the business.

 This is not a textbook, but the reader should be able to correctly answer the following multiple-choice question after reading it:

Which of the following has the greatest impact on changes in the valuation of investment real estate?

A   The anticipated increase or decrease in the cash flow.

B   The balance between the number of qualified buyers vs. the number of properties on the market.

C   Changes in yields of competing investments such as stocks and bonds.

D   The reduction or increase in the risk of collecting the future income stream.

{ **H**INT: The answer is contained in Annotations: 65 – The Relative Changes in the Prices of Investment } Real Estate are Most Influenced By. (You can refer to this section but the reader should know the answer after reading the investor narratives.)

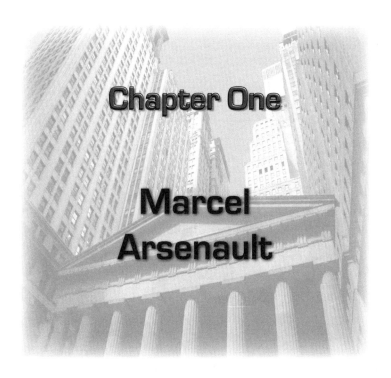

Chapter One

Marcel Arsenault

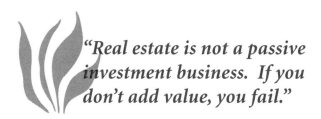

"Real estate is not a passive investment business. If you don't add value, you fail."

WE ADDED VALUE.

Adding **value means proactive leasing, careful property management, and** aggressive rent collection. We almost failed because we didn't understand these fundamentals.

ACHIEVEMENT HIGHLIGHTS

- Entrepreneur at an early age

- Early interest in biological systems

- Pursued Ph.D. in molecular biology

- Left academia to start food business

- Sold business to Beatrice Foods

- Invested proceeds in real estate

- Built team of 150 employee/partners

- Built multi-million dollar portfolio

- Founded two charitable foundations

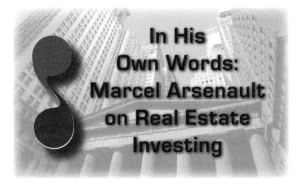

On Early Beginnings

I was an entrepreneurial youngster in Northern Quebec, in a strange mining town called Chibaugamu, a Cree Indian name.

I was an industrious kid. As a 12-year-old, I collected bottles and turned them in for a penny each. I also did some baby-sitting. I also loved to think about how things could work better, especially biological systems.

I was admitted to medical school but instead, pursued a Ph.D. in molecular biology at the University of Colorado, which had a world-class program. I actually turned down a chance to work with a scientist who won the Nobel Prize in order to participate in this program. I guess I've made some strange choices.

On Entrepreneurial Zeal

The University of Colorado program was great, but I still found time to start a business. My experience with my father's ice cream company led me to launch my own ice cream business. It was an early version of Ben & Jerry's—I was very progressive. At work I would fight like hell to keep my business afloat in the midst of a pit of raging alligators. At night I would study about humans and systems and how things worked.

Completing my Ph.D. and running a company eventually proved to be too much. So I chose to go the business route because I found more challenges in business than in the lab. Business is brutally forged on the great anvil of success. Science is not nearly as concrete or dynamic. You can be a minor professor in the bio world and survive just fine. But the business world is much tougher—you can't hide when you are running a company. Your performance is clearly measured by your ability to make business survive in a very competitive market. There are no seniority safety nets in business, nor is tenure a factor in measuring accomplishment. The options for the entrepreneur are success or failure.

We got into yogurt after about ten years. We built the company up and sold it to one of the largest conglomerates, Beatrice Foods, in the 1980s. I stayed on for a year as acting president, and they paid me a large sum of money. My receptionist back then, Pam, is running the company now and I talk to her once in a while. We joke about how she is doing better than I am.

When I sold my business, I had a lot of money in my pocket. At first I wanted to retire and write a book. I moved to Europe and started a new life. I remember running a spreadsheet that forecasted if I invested in real estate and stayed patient I could make a great return over a long period of time. I was looking for a new challenge, and once I got back to the U.S., I started putting my money to work.

On Early Real Estate Investing

I DECIDED TO DIVE INTO THE BOULDER, COLORADO REAL ESTATE MARKET. I had a theory that you should not live too far away from your properties. If there is a problem, you need to understand the merits of the marketplace. You need to know about the local economy and what is going on around you. Plus, if you live close to your property, you are going to get to know it better. Meet your customers so you know what is going on.

My initial focus in real estate investing was to purchase properties where an active and astute investor could boost the income stream. Those situations involve more risk but offer higher potential returns. I always thought for the long term, but there is no point in buying passive real estate if you are looking for higher yields. When I started investing I did not want to be burdened with low yields.

> There is no point buying passive real estate if you are looking for higher yields.

I could not have picked a worse time to start my foray into real estate. It was the top of the market when I entered the business in the mid 1980s. I was investing like those who dove into buying NASDAQ stocks when the index was 5,000.

I always thought real estate was passive, but I quickly found out that mostly it is not. There are passive real estate investments such as properties with long term leases signed by tenants with substantial credit. I have bought some Wal-Marts and those are passive. I visited one Wal-Mart and ran into the manager who could not believe you can buy a Wal-Mart.

"When will I see you?" the manager asked.

"In 19 years when your lease is up." I was willing to be patient.

 Job losses occurred in the Denver MSA in 1985 and 1986. For more on the Denver job situation post 1986 see Annotations: 54, Page 217 – Job Loss Stats in the Denver Area.

So back in the mid-1980s when I invested most of my money, the real estate market fell off a cliff. The national savings and loan scandal was roaring and I was at the vortex. All of a sudden real estate became a higher risk business than I had originally perceived. You had to beat the competition. It was difficult to get loans and it was hard to keep old tenants and get new ones. Lease rates were plummeting.

But through all of this I was working my ass off and stayed afloat. Being active, I did find a few good deals. We were smart about real estate, but a willingness to work hard was the difference. Our leasing authorities would sign leases on the hood of a car. We had very cheap pricing, we met with people on Sundays, and we took chances on a tenant, unlike a lot of the banks at the time.

On Success in Real Estate Investing

A FUNNY THING HAPPENED ON THE WAY TO SURVIVAL—WE FOUND SUCCESS. We found that the entire industry did not understand cash flow. I think we were among the first. Assume there is a building and the asking price is $9 million—most real estate investors understood that. But, at the time, since most of the assets were decreasing in value, potential buyers presumed that the erosion would continue. The key is not projecting the problems of the past, but looking at the future and how cash flow could be increased. When I first got started in the business, this concept of anticipating the future was drowned in a sea of pessimism. Having run the ice cream and yogurt business where current and future cash flow are critical, I knew how to analyze and identify future opportunity.

I discovered and figured out how to improve real estate cash flows early on. This was an industry that was asset oriented but not cash flow ori-

Anticipated increases in cash flow usually result in upward price pressure. See Annotations: 1, Page 129 – What are the Factors That Influence a Change in the Value of a Property?

ented. It was built on the Greater Fool Theory. Instead of developing property for long-term cash flow, they were developed for a quick profit. At the time, most investors and developers were focused on hard assets and construction costs. I focused on effective leasing and cash flow.

We would hang banners on buildings offering below market lease rates. We were able to do this because our acquisition pricing and structuring allowed us that luxury. We would have our people go to neighborhoods or go to small businesses and drum up some tenants. We kept in touch with city zoning people, who knew about the guys working out of their garages who were getting licenses to start new businesses. We would approach him and make him a tenant.

The strategy was obvious, but it took a long, long time to bear fruit. We built our entire business by buying failed properties and finding creative ways to fill them up. It was like a pie-eating contest—we could not buy them fast enough. We were involved with Silverado Properties from George W. Bush's brother, Neil. We were paying 11 cents on the loan dollar in transactions we bought from the FDIC.

Many investors have had success buying property below construction costs. Annotations: 15, Page 159– Buying Investment Real Estate Below Construction Costs.

A lot of these buildings were half-empty. Most had either little or no cash flow, so we had to become adept at filling these properties with tenants. We really worked on managing the business. I wasn't looking for astronomical growth. Instead, I wanted steady growth with well-managed properties. We didn't want to flip properties. We had to adapt to a tremendously difficult environment, and became very sharp at buying distressed properties.

WHEN WE STARTED OUT WE SAID WE WOULD OWN PROPERTIES FOREVER AND PAY OFF THE MORTGAGE. But the economy was in distress, so we were undergoing economic distress, too. I looked at our properties from a portfolio perspective. There were times when part of the portfolio had to be sold to allow us to devote capital and people to other more important assets.

The most critical part of our strategy was our understanding and our commitment to creative leasing. We learned, and when necessary, conceived numerous techniques to keep buildings occupied. This was during a time when other owners, even institutional ones, could not keep their buildings full. It was all about acting entrepreneurial, clearing the red tape, and making it easy and affordable for people to lease our properties.

The Chinese proverb about opportunity originating from problems was our mantra. The market went down and we worked hard.

> Flipping a property is a buyer's dream, executed to the detriment of the seller. Annotations: 61 Page 228 - Flipping a Property.

Then the market moved back up and we could use what we had learned to do even better. Most real estate investors did not survive that period.

On Early Acquisitions

ONE OF MY FIRST DEALS involved the purchase of a complex of four office buildings in Denver. The price was $1,276,000 with $176,000 down and an acquisition loan of $1,100,000. I was attracted to the property as a result of a combination of attractive price and our ability to add value. It was a workout property that had high vacancy. In addition, some of the construction, such as interior finish, had not been completed.

Offering free rent is the most common method used to induce a tenant to rent space. For more leasing ideas go to Annotations: 32 Page 192 – Leasing Ideas and Promotions.

To maximize the value of the investment we finished the interior space, primarily a raw slab upon acquisition. We also started an intensive in-house leasing and management program. Our ability to undercut the competition on lease rates was due to our low acquisition cost. As part of the acquisition, we obtained a construction loan to complete the workout.

We took a very entrepreneurial approach to both management and leasing. Our leasing agents were given authority to sign leases on the spot. Our in-house construction teams facilitated quick move-in for new tenants.

We sold one of the four buildings for $765,000 to a tenant who had an option to purchase in their lease. Of the three remaining buildings, we sold one for $760,000 and the last two sold for a combined price of $2,275,000. We exchanged out of each of those buildings into other properties. From the initial investment of $176,000, our final profit after all improvements and costs was over $2,000,000.

Evolving Investment Strategies

An important aspect of real estate investing is to understand how to change investment strategy during market shifts. My investment goals have been modified as the market changed. Initially we purchased only value-added or workout properties with high yield and high internal rates of return.

It's important to understand how to change investment strategy during market shifts.

That was my strategy from the mid-1980s until 1993. From 1993 to 2003, which we perceived to be the peak of the market, we sold 30 percent of our original local portfolio and exchanged it into stable, long-term net-leased properties with nationwide locations. Now we are selling some stable, net-leased portfolios that we will exchange once again into more high-return, value-added deals.

It is important to exercise astute portfolio management. See Annotations: 16, Page 161 – Portfolio Management.

Although the investment plan has changed, I have

always kept what I believe are the best located, most competitive buildings in my portfolio. We still own nearly two-thirds of the local buildings we purchased from 1988 to 1993.

On The Power of People

IT BOILS DOWN TO PEOPLE. Most developers and investors know property better than I do. I was a biologist. But I do know people. I know how to train them and work shoulder-to-shoulder with them. Unlike most real estate people, I don't know all the facets of the buildings and their physical structure. I care less about buildings and more about putting together a team that understands the relationship between the physical structure and the business practices that must be executed to have the investment make sense.

> The IRR is the rate of return. To see how it is calculated, go to Annotations: 58, Page 224.

People who say one particular corner location makes a property work astounds me. Location is important, but not as significant as having the right people assisting you in determining the right strategy that contributes to the ability to generate current and future cash flow. It's all about making the right people your partners.

It's not location, location, location. It does matter,

but it is already built into the price. If you have a good location, all that means is that you have a property whose location creates part of the value. But if you don't have great management and great people you won't survive. That's what we did in surviving those bad times—I was able to work with people and empower them and harness their talent. I even learned from them. If you focus on people and not buildings you'll do fine.

I have put a lot of sweat equity into employees. I wanted them to think like entrepreneurs. I liked "A" personalities who wanted to learn about real estate. I found that they were dedicated and acted like owners instead of just employees. We built a team of 150 people who have now been with us for 10 to 15 years.

Even today, I have an okay understanding of properties, but there are probably 200 people in Colorado who know more than I do about the physical product of real estate. But I knew that people were always the key.

I remember a broker named Peter Wells. About 10 years ago, I was sitting on the floor in the office on a Sunday putting together loan packages.

The phone rang and it was Peter. "Hey, I hope you don't mind my calling you," he said. "I've been watching you and I think you are doing things the right way." He wanted to talk about some deals. So I put him on

Employee bonuses must be awarded on the basis of measurable, quantifiable goals. Annotations: 13, Page 155 - Employee Compensation Plans.

speakerphone and I grew impressed. He sounded like he knew what he was doing. He took the time to get to know me and how I work, so I decided to meet him.

We started looking at deals together. Over the next five years, he sold me a great deal of property. He found out what I liked and what I needed. I grew to trust him, which is why we did business together.

> The ability of a broker to 'add value' is a function of their familiarity with the market, their capability of accessing information, their ability to see value where others don't, their ability to find properties for sale and their potential for sourcing buyers. Annotations: 4, Page 135 – Selecting the Right Broker.

I might have intrigued him, but the funny thing is, we got along as partners and not as a client and a broker. I asked him to find things we could team up and work on together. "I'll think about that," he said.

A few months later he found a property that used to be a condo and had been rehabbed. We decided to turn the deal back into a condo. It was about 20 miles away. Peter presented me the deal and sent me the numbers. I decided to go for it.

He asked me to swing by and see the property. I declined. I told him that he was the one who knew condos and not me. Sure, I was putting up most of the money, but Peter knew the deal. I was betting on him, not the building.

He said that was unusual. I told him I could get the financing from the bank and I was ready to write a check. I did that part, and asked him to do most of the rest. There were a few false starts, but the project wound up doing well and we both made a lot of money. After that, I bought apartments that he would then buy from me and turn into condos.

Increased demand makes conversion of apartments to condominiums popular. Annotations: 20, Page 172 - Conversion of Apartments to Condominiums.

We have done more than $250 million of business together and now he is a rich man. We went out for a beer recently and he told me what he was worth. I shook his hand. We were both very happy. But I pointed out it wasn't due to me, as he was suggesting. He was the guy who did all the hard work.

Peter, like many brokers (but not all), thinks like an entrepreneur. Brokers are contractors who have to earn everything they get. So we're bringing more brokers into these deals. We are both in our fifties and we want to keep it going. Our formula of investing and profit sharing is creating many new opportunities.

It is important to hire competent new employees who can learn at the arm of an experienced practitioner. The added expense will be rewarded. Annotations: 12 Page 154 - Suggestions on Building an Internal Staff.

On Building Real Estate Wealth

WE ARE SEEDING AND FEEDING THE RIGHT PEOPLE, young people who love real estate, who will work hard and find good deals. I think my primary strong point is that even if I do not necessarily know when to buy and sell real estate, I do know how to recognize talent.

What I may lack in various facets of real estate management, I make up for by knowing how to find good people and how to help them learn about real estate from the perspective of the cash flow-oriented entrepreneurial investor. I want them to know going in that real estate is very hard work that requires a total commitment to learning and executing certain fundamentals.

Real estate requires a total commitment to learning and executing certain fundamentals.

But if they do work hard, my people learn the true secrets of real estate investing. They gain the ability to see opportunity where others see risk. They learn how to reduce risk through sound management and property marketing. They learn how to increase cash flow while balancing the relationship of leverage to risk. They learn how to identify certain market cycles and what strategy to use during those market fluctuations. Ultimately and most importantly, they learn the value of the people with whom they work.

 ## Other Thoughts

I was always interested in how the brain works and why and how humans are what they are. This gave me a chance to develop my nonprofit foundations later in life. It also influenced my personal belief that humans need to move beyond war in order to get along and live together.

Globalization makes me think it will happen. The purpose of these two foundations over the next 100 years will be to help humankind finish the gluing process, so that we all stick together.

I think about how far the world has already come. The United States was originally just disjointed territories. Italy was the same way, with its provinces at war with each other. Now you have NAFTA and the European Union. Because I have always been intellectually curious about how systems work, I naturally integrated it into my business ventures.

 ## Personal

Still holding onto his long-standing theory that real estate investors should not live too far away from their properties, Marcel Arsenault resides in Superior, Colorado, where he is CEO of Colorado and Santa Fe Real Estate, which manages a rapidly growing global real estate portfolio. He is also the founder and chairman of the Arsenault Family Foundation and the

Ending War Foundation.

Current local market holdings include twelve office buildings, fifteen retail buildings, seven industrial buildings, six miscellaneous buildings including some residential holdings, and fourteen single tenant net-leased investments scattered throughout the United States.

Further Reading

See the following Annotations on other office building development and ownership topics:

Annotations: 31, Page 191 - Financing the Typical Suburban Office Development Project.

Annotations: 33, Page 194 - What Constitutes a Favorable Location for New Suburban Office Development?

Annotations: 34, Page 195 - Owning and Operating Multi-tenant Office Buildings.

Chapter Two

Ben Leeds

"I always liked the idea that people could give me something and I could make more from it."

I AM PRIMARILY
AN APARTMENT INVESTOR

The multifamily segment is more definable, more predictable ... a necessary commodity and more responsive to effective management.

ACHIEVEMENT HIGHLIGHTS

- Started four businesses by age fifteen

- Employed six people in high school

- Learned to hire good people early

- Funded college from business ventures

- Introduced to real estate in college

- Gave up medical school to sell real estate

- Started his own brokerage company

- Closed company to focus on investing

- Accumulated multi-million dollar portfolio

An Early Entrepreneur

A lot of my story has been driven by the moves I made early in my life, and helps give some perspective on what it takes to be successful in real estate.

I feel that you are either an entrepreneur or not. In real estate, it takes an independent mind to make the investments, make deals, and consummate transactions.

> In real estate, it takes an independent mind to make the investments, make deals, and consummate transactions.

I started in first grade. Everyone met in homeroom with his or her lunch money. I was the one at the grocery store, loading up with candy at 15 cents a bar, hopping the fence, and selling the candy bars in homeroom for 50 cents.

That was the beginning for me. I found early on you could take a small investment and make money on it.

When I was 11 years old I had a Playboy Clubhouse. We had Playboy Magazines. My friends loved it. They made it a point to get money from their parents to join the Playboy Clubhouse, although I doubt they mentioned the name of the club when they were hitting up their parents for the cash. To my friends it was a hip thing to do—to join my Playboy Clubhouse.

I liked the idea of making something out of nothing. I always liked the idea that people could give me something and I could make more from it, like my Playboy Clubhouse—it yielded a return.

I didn't have a father figure. My mom was an English teacher. My dad was out of the scene. I wasn't getting a pat on the back from a male role model, but if I could make money on a deal, I considered that pat in the back.

Between grade school and junior high, I started two other businesses, both of which were profitable.

When I was 14 years old, I used my money from my other businesses to go out and buy my first car, an old Toyota Land Cruiser, three on the stick shift, all beaten up. I didn't even have a learner's permit. I'd have my mom or someone drive me to go and get new parts so I could rehab the vehicle and turn it around to sell it for a big profit.

I loved classic cars. I bought and restored Jaguars, Porsches, Corvettes, Mustangs, even rust buckets. I made a big profit on all of them.

Then I started a business where I would do a 20-point car inspection, checking the brakes and compression and test driving the vehicles for drivers. If people were buying a car and wanted to know the quality of the car, they could bring the car to us. If we found something wrong with the car, we could get our clients a discount.

From that experience, I learned the importance of hiring people and delegating. I always seemed to work better with my mind than my hands. I had about six guys working for me on the car inspection project.

My favorite part of all of this was negotiating for a better price on a car using the Blue Book, or maybe taking an old car and fixing it up and getting a higher return on investment. The car business lasted through most of my college years. My favorite part of the transaction was negotiating the contract and price.

I realized my favorite part of the transaction was negotiating the contract and price.

On Entering the Real Estate Business

I noticed that some of my clients, and my brother, were negotiating bigger contracts and bigger prices in real estate—without getting their hands dirty. So, I went out and got my license for real estate. I was in pre-med in college but lost interest in becoming a doctor.

As part of my introduction to investment real estate, I worked at two different commercial real estate brokerage companies, both of which were major competitors in my local market. Their training and the brokerage experience was essential for me. You need a strong foundation to succeed in real estate, especially when it comes to being a good decision maker.

I became top producer for one of the leading local brokerage companies.

After several years in investment brokerage, I again saw that my brother was having parallel success. We took a big leap and started our own commercial brokerage company. I was 28 years old at the time and was risking my considerable success in brokering investment real estate by taking management duties. My brother was a partner, along with a couple of other real estate professionals who knew their way around, all top producers. We ended up having over 40 agents working for us.

Beginning in 1990, our market turned upside down. My talents were the wheeling and dealing with investment transactions. I shouldn't have gotten caught up in management of a brokerage company. I found out the hard way that I should have been out on my own. I left the brokerage company a few years later.

It is highly taxing owning and managing a brokerage company versus being an investor. Wearing many hats is a diluting and compromising thing to do.

I found out the hard way that I should have been out on my own.

On Investment Real Estate Concepts and Trends

In 1990 I went back to buying property for myself and selling it for a profit. The timing was good because the market was in decline. My area of specialty was investing in "C" and "B" quality properties. As background, I rank the various real estate property grades from "A" to "F."

Taking into account the types of property and the evolving real estate cycles, my goal is to minimize risk while maintaining the greatest opportunity for enhancing value. This is easier said than done, but by following certain basic concepts, I have been able to grow my portfolio not only in the up, but also in the down cycles.

I am primarily an apartment investor since the multifamily segment is for me more definable, more predictable—a necessary commodity and more responsive to effective management. It is also the easiest to finance, which is an important part of accelerating the growth of your real estate portfolio.

Generally speaking, if a property yields a higher initial return, it is usually a result of a greater perceived risk. Higher perceived risk is linked to lower prices. The opportunity is in finding deals where the perceptions of most competing investors are

The opportunity is in finding deals where the perceptions of most competing investors are wrong.

wrong.

If an investor can increase cash flow beyond what the existing owner has been able to generate, the opportunity for appreciation can be multiplied exponentially. However, the change in cash flow is not the only variable affecting value. In today's market, prices have been going up primarily because there has been an imbalance between buyers and sellers, with the sellers being a minority. Cash flow is still important, but the balance between buyers and sellers also impacts pricing.

> Property value is influenced by risk; cash flow; buyer and seller imbalances; and competing investments. See Annotations: 1 Page 129 - What Are the Factors That Influence a Change in the Value of a Property?

An investor has to look at the property level as well as the market level to predict changes in cash flow and overall value. Some investors will take lower current cash flows because they perceive their short and long term risk is lower. Low risk and long-term appreciation are motivators for many investors.

Through astute acquisitions and effective management, an investor does not necessarily have to sacrifice low short-term cash flow. But even that concept can be overwhelmed by a flood of investors looking for a limited number of properties on the market.

We are in a similar market right now (2005)— fairly inflated, with more buyers than sellers and people buying for appreciation. That's a bad thing because property values almost always decline due to higher interest rates, which results in lower cash flow. A market that is fueled by overactive buyers can lead to future down cycles. As cash flow gets squeezed, the appreciation stops and we go into a declining market. Not only does cash flow go down, but the perception of real estate compared to other investments can be negatively impacted. When the buyers disappear and cash flows are eroding, the market can change to the negative very quickly. It is my belief that in mid-2005 we are heading there. Nothing happens overnight, but all the indicators are in place.

> **A market that is fueled by overactive buyers can lead to future down cycles.**

Choosing the Right Apartments for Portfolio Growth

Assume you are buying an "A" apartment property in an "A" location. To buy such a property, you would have to pay a premium price. Properties with premium prices usually have proportionally lower cash flow and, depending on the financing, could have little or no cash flow. Such properties also command high rents. There are some disadvantages with high rent properties. First, almost all new construction projects are of high quality and compete for the high rent seg-

The rental market competes with the after tax costs of home ownership. See Annotations: 26 Page 179 – Simple Analysis Techniques for Forecasting Apartment Rental Trends.

ment of the tenant market. This type of renter is not the largest part of the market. Oversupply in this segment can occur very rapidly, negatively affecting cash flow and value. In addition to competing for a smaller population, tenants who pay higher rent are typically the ones that are more capable of purchasing a home or condo. In low-interest rate markets, especially in markets with high home affordability ratios, the loss of renters to ownership can be significant. So, in addition to competing with other "A" apartment projects for this tenant, the entire home sale market is also a competitor.

Those are the reasons why I usually buy a "B" or "C" quality property. With such properties I don't have to command a very high rent. There will always be a market for my property based on the formula for supply and demand. Supply is usually fixed since the higher costs of new construction preempt new projects from charging rents that compete with my market segment. There is a much higher demand for basic rent that the masses can afford.

That formula means my rent would be far more stable and have lower risk than rent on an "A" property that, in essence, is a luxury item, and could fluctuate dramatically.

 On Market Timing

In the declining market of late 1994 and early 1995, investor opportunities were abundant although there were many who were looking back as opposed to looking forward. Apartment buildings were yielding very high cash flows and there was a flood of inventory, compliments of the Resolution Trust Corporation and bank foreclosures. Also, there were relatively few buyers as a result of concerns about further market declines.

Banks were flooded with defaulted properties. It was a great opportunity for people who had cash. For some existing owners there were deals that could be negotiated with banks, whereby the bank would reduce their loan payments or in some cases, the principal amounts, so that the borrower would not walk away from the property. This turned negative cash flow properties into cash positive. I was the beneficiary of such situations.

At the time, I also owned several commercial properties and did not lose one. In spite of experimenting with office and retail property ownership, my primary emphasis was in apartments—in fact, I was aggressively acquiring properties at the time when others were going under. I was seeing returns at 20-30 percent for "C" or "B" property. Compare that to today, when you would be happy to get a 5 percent return on a "C" property.

> A changing market is when the most money is made and lost.

> **A rapidly rising market is often an excellent time to trade up to higher quality buildings. Annotations: 22 Page 174 – Market Pricing Portfolio Options for Apartment Investors.**

As the old Chinese curse goes, may you live in interesting times. In real estate, a changing market is when the most money is made, or for some investors, when the most is lost.

For example, in my opinion, the current market (mid-2005) is not a good time to buy properties; it is a good time to sell. Interest rates are going up. Cash flow yield is the lowest we have seen since 1989 and my feeling is that people who are buying for cash flow in today's market will get hurt.

So, the 1990s were turning out to be pretty good for me. Opportunities came up, and my goal was to aggressively buy as much as I could get my hands on. The returns were fantastic.

On Building a Management Team

I didn't plan to own a management company, but I was buying so many properties that I found myself having to micro-manage at the property level. I wound up writing my own checks and doing my own bills, doing my own repairs and maintenance. I realized that my greatest ability to create value was in finding and negotiating the best deals not doing repairs and maintenance. I learned to delegate work out to crews and I had my management company to run the buildings. My main focus now is to find investments and buy and sell in anticipation of market cycles. I delegate property management deals to my staff.

> **Your portfolio must be large enough to justify hiring full time employees. Off-site management needs senior management focus. Annotations: 10 Page 150 – In-House Off Site Property Management Issues.**

Most real estate investors will tell you that creating a good staff is the toughest thing to do. I agree. Until 2002, I was still aggressively buying, which I'd been doing since 1995. My biggest dilemma has always been handling what I am acquiring. The biggest hindrance for me was being intimidated about buying because of problems managing my firm and my crews. So I try to keep up by continually upgrading management staff. It means a lot of hiring, training, delegating, and sometimes firing.

For my management company, I looked for a strong controller and a strong off-site management team. Management is an evolving process. Personnel changes should be thought through, but compromise in key positions will almost always lead to trouble. You are always fine-tuning a real

> **You should put in place a long term compensation plan for your management team. Annotations: 10, Page 150 - In-House Off Site Property Management Issues.**

> The number one method for attracting prospective tenants has been for-rent signs posted on the project.
> Annotations: 27, Page 181 – Best Methods of Sourcing Apartment Renters.

estate business. Employees with poor attitudes or those who are not contributing to the team should be eliminated. In a tough business such as ours, you need high morale and positive environment. If my managers are not treating their people with respect, it is time to make a change. Morale will improve after such decisions are made.

The business of property management is a thankless job. Tenants are never happy, things are not getting fixed well enough, and your property managers want more support and resources. The ability of the on-site team to optimize the balance between revenue and expenses is truly an art. As an owner, you have to understand the opportunities and the risks.

On Partners

In addition to the constant headaches of property management, you may have some partners in your deals. The partners' goals may not be consistent with what the property needs are in terms of reinvestment. There are periods during the evolution of a property when capital repairs are necessary. Sometimes cash flow has to be tempered to make necessary physical improvements. Partners are not necessarily astute enough to understand this fact or other issues that may come up. You can try to accommodate everyone, but your understanding of how the property should operate should not be preempted by short term partner needs. My Granddad said, "If partners were such a good idea, God would have one."

As an early investor in real estate, I found myself in need of pulling in partners because it was the best way to raise the cash that I needed to get the deals done. But ideally you want as few partners as possible. I still have partners, mostly family members, but try to keep it at a minimum.

On Selling vs. Holding

BIG LESSON: I REGRET EVERYTHING I HAVE EVER SOLD. Nothing has kept up with the value of real estate. The reasons to sell might include a deteriorating local market, the need to diversify out of a particular area, or to take a profit if some insane buyer wants to offer much more than a property might be worth. With that as background, why I sold and what I sold made sense at the time, but I still regret selling—it was a means to an end. A better process is to refinance and reinvest the proceeds in other investment property. The refinance is a tax-free event. The costs are minimal and there is no rush to reinvest the proceeds. While the dollar is becoming more and more worthless, our real estate becomes worth more and more.

When it's hard to find a good deal as a buyer, it's a great time to sell. Any investor considering getting out of the market for whatever reason should consider the environment in mid-2005 as a peak. Nevertheless, I am not selling. I just enjoy the business too much. I'm young and can take the abuse.

On Staying Local – Unless?

In 2003 I saw our market changing. Prices were getting high and yield was going down. So my acquisitions were being reduced. Maybe instead of ten at a time I was doing only five.

In 2005, I have gone from five escrows to today having one or two. It's a weird feeling. But I was not finding good deals. And, I don't want to have to work hard and take on greater risk of losing money.

Since I am a hard-core deal junkie, in order for me to find good investments, for the first time in my investment career I am looking for deals out of my own area. I have always believed real estate is a local business requiring local knowledge and local proximity to react

> Third party, off-site managers are usually good at getting business and executing it in the short term. Annotations: 9, Page 147 – Off-Site Management: In House vs. Third Party Vendors.

to and solve problems. Maybe reason will overcome my need to make a deal and I will resist the out-of-area temptation. The one thing to avoid in buying deals out of your market is to buy small deals that cannot financially support professional third-party management.

 ## On Creating Your Reputation as a Real Estate Investor

One of my most recent purchases was a $14.5 million apartment investment. I saw some offers that were $500,000 more than my offer. Mine was all cash, with a quick close escrow that was not contingent. That means I wasn't being picky about inspections and things that may or may not have been okay with property—an as-is deal. The seller saw the value of that —it was worth more than $500,000 to get the deal done.

I try to make that my goal as an investor. It creates an environment where people say, "That Ben Leeds, he is a solid player. We want to do the deal with him." Reputation in this business is so important.

Since I started as an agent in this business, I know that brokers are focused on their commissions. I want them to

If you are always trying to negotiate a fee with a broker, he or she will probably not have you at the top of their deal list.

know that when they bring me a deal, the probability of closing is high and that their fee is secure. If you are always trying to negotiate a fee with a broker, he or she will probably not have you at the top of their list when it comes to seeing deals that may be for sale. If you are a serious and a repeat investor, you should have a good relationship with the brokerage community.

When you are a broker, or an agent, you do a deal and you get your commission. End of story. That's how I started in the business—making clients a lot of money. They continually made more money because they got the appreciated value of the property, plus they received the continuing cash flow of the property. Meanwhile, I was not getting any of that money until I got another brokerage deal. That's why I like the role of a principal owning apartment buildings—money is always coming in, plus you get the benefit of profits on sale, taxed at capital gains rates.

> I like the role of a principal owning apartment buildings— money is always coming in.

On Lessons in Building Your Portfolio

LOOK FOR A STABLE ENVIRONMENT WITH AN EMPHASIS ON JOB GROWTH and hopefully some limitations on supply. Limits on supply can be such things as lack of developable land or city politics that are adverse to development.

I am primarily a Los Angeles investor. Oxnard, California has had better pricing and is close enough to the Los Angeles market that I could be a hands-on investor. With rising costs and values you have to look out of your standard buying parameters, or you will be boxed in without

> There are several factors to consider when evaluating relative apartment market strength. Annotations: 24, Page 176 – Analyzing Apartment Markets.

future growth of investments to acquire. Because of limited growth and high demand, it is a very attractive area. You can buy with a good cash flow. Tenant demand is very high, so Oxnard and the surrounding areas are booming.

Be a hands-on manager. As far as investments go, I am a hands-on investor. You cannot be an in-between.

Get a real estate license. Anyone who wants to invest in real estate should have a license. You may not use it but it can be an educational tool that will allow you to see the latest trends in the brokerage business.

As a beginner, you will rely on other people, so rely on people who are in the business for a living. Join your local owner associations. Get to know and exchange ideas with the top investment real estate brokers in your area. To keep up on financing you should be in contact with the top lenders and mortgage brokers. Total immersion in your product and being an information junkie are two of the keys to success. Get involved in the Multiple Listing Service of your area.

Every apartment investor should know and have a list of vendors. See Annotations: 23, Page 175 - Apartment Investor Vendor List.

Apartment investors should know and have a list of vendors in their Rolodex. The list should include: the three to five most active apartment brokers in their area; an experienced real estate attorney; an accountant familiar with the tax aspects of real estate ownership; the three to five most active apartment mortgage brokers; a building contractor who is familiar with multi-family construction.

It helps to learn the business from the bottom up. I have a five-year-old son. I'd love to get him into this business. If I had my druthers, I would have him paint apartments and then do plumbing and electrical work. Then, I'd have him become a property inspector for vacancies, move-outs, and finally do on-site renting of apartments so he can see different aspects of business. Then, I would get him into administration so he could gain proficiency in that area. He would need to be familiar with all aspects of the business. The more training you get in real estate investment, the better you know what a good deal is. You can't learn that unless you are in the trenches, eating, sleeping, and breathing apartment buildings and real estate transactions. You can then see trends and where the market is going, you get comparable sales information to help determine value, you will get to understand return on investment, and you will be aware of what has happened in the last six months since you know your own financial reporting.

Remember, this business is more than today's numbers. Real estate trades on future assumptions of income growth or contraction. Your ability to anticipate future cash flow should dramatically influence the financial structuring you do today.

When working with lenders, today's numbers are more important than future projections. Most lenders base their loans on today's numbers with sometimes some small allowances for future changes.

On Current Holdings

Ben currently owns 75 separate apartment projects totaling over 1,600 units with a market value of over $160,000,000.

Further Reading

See the following Annotations on other topics relating to investing in and managing apartments:

Annotations: 28, Page 183 - Guarding Against Resident Manager Fraud.
Annotations: 29, Page 186 - Resident Managers—Can They Sell?

Annotations: 30, Page 189 - Determining Apartment Rental Rates.

Annotations: 62, Page 229 - Unsolicited Offers.

Leeds

Chapter Three

John Hamilton

"Growing up gave me a different perspective of the world, of having a plastic spoon, rather than a silver one, in your mouth."

I WILL BUY A COMMERCIAL TRACT IN FRONT OF A SUBDIVISION

where I can put a grocery store and assorted other tenants who can provide products and services to the nearby homeowners.

ACHIEVEMENT HIGHLIGHTS

✦ Early interest in real estate

✦ Learned early which jobs to avoid

✦ Business success before real estate

✦ Identified new opportunities in
real estate development

✦ Tested by and survived worst
market in fifty years

✦ From modest start, big ups
and downs before success

✦ Found right markets, right
products, and right formulas

✦ Built portfolio of over $200 million

On His Early Interests and Endeavors

I grew up in a working class neighborhood of Boston, the sixth of seven children. My father worked for Singer Sewing Machine Co. in the textile industry and my mother took care of the house. Growing up in that atmosphere gave me a different perspective of the world, one of having a plastic spoon, rather than a silver one in your mouth. At the age of six, my father died, leaving my mother with the responsibility of caring and feeding our large family. We all learned responsibility very quickly and carried on. At an early age, I had dreams of building houses. I used to get up early to sketch houses on a pad to see

I used to get up early to sketch houses on a pad to see the different ways of building them.

the different ways of building them. At the age of 15, being driven to succeed and to make my parents proud was my goal. I knew then that I wanted to go into real estate. I was determined to become a builder of the houses in my sketch pads.

After graduating from high school, I left Boston with my family to move to Florida. I attended Hillsboro Community College in Tampa, Florida for one year. Quickly it became apparent that college could not keep my attention, and after hearing about job opportunities in the fast-growing Houston area from a school friend, I relocated to Texas in the early 1970s.

As a nineteen year old lacking alternatives for higher paying jobs, I started in the construction industry. My school friend lived in Houston and always talked about Brown and Root, an international oil-industry engineering company based there. He said we could get jobs paying $10 an hour, which we did. I started out as a journeyman iron worker and then became a project foreman. After five years, it was obvious that there was no room for advancement, so I left with lots of knowledge, insight, and experience to venture out on my own.

On Entrepreneurial Beginnings

While I was working in Houston, one of my brothers died in the line of duty while serving for the United States Marine Corps. He left my mom $20,000 from his life insurance policy, which from my perspective at that time, was more money than God could ever print. Mom loaned me $5,000 that I invested in a painting business. I called it Calvin Bruce Paint Industries, named after my late brother Bruce, and my deceased brother-in-law, Calvin. Focusing on contract work for local apartment developers, I built Calvin Bruce Paint from three employees into a 160-person operation.

In spite of the success of Calvin Bruce Paint, I realized at the end of every month when looking at the money food chain of the company, I was the last to get paid. The employees were paid hourly as the job progressed and I usually got paid after the job was completed. I figured that I could move up much further in the pay line by going after my life-long goal of developing real estate. As a developer, I would be the person cutting the checks to the vendors. It was at that time that I sold my painting firm and entered with vigor into the world of developing apartment complexes.

On His First Venture into Real Estate Development

Based on my experience of watching developers build apartment complexes, I began my new venture by constructing two small apartment complexes in Pasadena, Texas. My plan was to go into less desirable parts of town with the hope of convincing banks to advance a loan in areas that they had previously red-lined. When I told the banks of my plan, their initial reaction was negative. Not one to take no for an answer along with pressure from the government to lend in those areas, they eventually talked to me. With my enthusiasm, a small personal investment and the

> My plan was to go into less desirable parts of town with the hope of convincing banks to advance a loan.

bank's money, I started building apartment complexes in some of the more challenging areas of Houston.

My early years were full of on-the-job training. Without classroom experience, there was a lot of trial and error. Although my apartment development business was making money, it was high risk. The ability to maintain the properties and collect rents was a constant challenge with the potential risk of substantial financial peril. I sold the apartment properties in order to build shopping centers which would be more lucrative. It was at that time that I started buying small commercial tracts of land in the Houston market that were in great demand with high growth potential.

The average asking rent in Houston is now almost double the average reported at the low point in 1987. Annotations: 55, Page 218 - Down Cycle in Houston.

The shopping center development business was booming and over a three year period, I built many shopping centers. The oil crunch in the Houston area hit and wiped everyone out. There were some major developers from all over that got crushed, and I did too. I woke up one morning with $11,000 in my bank account, down from millions. My silver spoon disappeared and the plastic one was back.

Despite my disaster in Houston, I still believed in my development formula. I just needed to find the right market. After much thought and thorough investigation, I found that Nashville, Tennessee, a great trucking Mecca, was doing very well economically. It was time to start over again. The formula worked in Nashville and my portfolio expanded rapidly. My positive experience in Nashville led to the development of shopping centers in Charlotte, North Carolina and Atlanta, Georgia. It took me five years, but I rebuilt my portfolio to one that was even larger than my earlier Houston, Texas holdings.

On Identifying Other Opportunities

As I was continuing on my journey out of Texas, I decided to do some new research on the Houston market. I found that the fundamentals of the development market were still weak, but I felt that the timing was right to investigate another opportunity. With my extensive background in the construction trades, I identified what I thought might be a significant value added business opportunity.

I began with the acquisition of small construction businesses such as plumbing and glass companies, forming them into a group. My strategy paid off, as I wound up being bought out by larger investors who wanted these companies to add to their portfolios. Between my successful shopping center

I wound up being bought out by larger investors who wanted these companies to add to their portfolios.

~ 57 ~

development activity and my profitable mergers and acquisitions, I found myself in a very desirable position. The dreaded plastic spoon was gone and the infamous silver spoon magically reappeared. After these successes, I decided to take up golf to occupy some of my time.

On Yet Another New Venture

I eventually grew tired of tee times, so I started to poke around the Houston development market again. In the process, I met my soon-to-be new partner. At the time, he was working on various projects for the city of Houston. He was younger than me and with his energy and enthusiasm, he rekindled my interest in developing real estate in Houston. This new partnership was formed in the 1990s and during that time we built a sizeable inventory of property. By 2003, the portfolio was quite large, and

> **My partner wanted to build, hold, rent, and manage the projects. It was my desire to build and sell.**

as it continued to grow, my partner wanted to build, hold, rent and manage the projects. It was my desire to build and sell. It was this difference in philosophy that led to our split, so I sold out my share to him and we continued to be friends.

Having gone through the 1980s and taking the

rental route was great at that time, but the economy downturn in Texas taught me a great lesson. You can't really survive a tough economy when you own and rent. Markets that can be overbuilt are fraught with inherent risk. A developer who is in the business of building and selling is in a less risky situation and the financial rewards are far greater.

On Current Additions to His Development Strategy

In 2004, I formed Option 1 Realty Group and with my investment strategies have built a $200 million asset base, with most of the hard assets in shopping centers in Texas, New Mexico and Arizona. There are also some high rise condo projects, but only in resort areas. With the good economy and low interest rates, Baby Boomers are looking for a place to retire or have a second home close to water, golf, and gaming. Those are the places I am looking to develop.

On Miscellaneous Recommendations

I prefer new growth areas around newer but not remote subdivisions. I will buy a commercial tract out in front of the subdivision where I can put a grocery store and assorted other tenants who can provide products and services to the nearby homeowners. My tenants attract customers that want the convenience of shopping near their home.

AVOID COMPROMISING YOUR TENANT BASE WITH FINANCIALLY UNSOUND OR UNCONVENTIONAL TENANTS. These type of tenants make a project difficult to finance and deter good tenants from wanting to place their business there as well. Good tenants attract other good tenants. Low quality tenants make a project much more difficult to sell. I cater to and seek tenants that have great stories about their past successes.

If leasing to weaker tenants, insist on personal guarantees. A competent real estate attorney should be employed to draft the proper personal guarantee language. The laws governing personal guarantees vary among states.

Location in the traffic path of residential developments is very important to retail projects. Annotations: 38, Page 200 – Suggestions on Owning Operating Convenience Retail Projects.

Signage is very important for retail developments, especially if catering to necessity and convenience shoppers. Annotations: 41, Page 205 – Sign Location and Visibility for Retail Projects.

Annotations: 39, Page 201 - Screening Noncredit Tenants.

AVOID SPECIALTY PURPOSE BUILDINGS. Specialty buildings are difficult to finance. They are difficult to re-lease in the event they become vacant. They are also usually more expensive to build. Finally, prospective buyers who will look at specialty buildings are a small number, which makes the project a harder sell, unless you want to discount your price.

DON'T DEVELOP IN SECONDARY LOCATIONS. Secondary locations are tempting because of the lower cost of land. The problem is that the land is at a lower cost for a reason. Finding tenants for sub-standard locations, especially for retail development projects, limits your ability to find worthy tenants.

Develop the highest quality project you can financially justify. Quality projects in quality locations usually attract higher quality tenants, more aggressive lenders, more aggressive buyers and more aggressive prices. Obviously the quality project still has to pencil out in terms of being economically viable, but at least you can use more optimistic assumptions of rents and valuations.

> The rent tenants will pay is typically somewhere between asking rents for comparable projects and rents in competing buildings. Annotations: 51, Page 215 – Determining Asking Rents.

Make sure that you have a high quality internal support staff. You live and die by your staff. Understaffing is a sure way to increase the risk of poor execution. You should always try to have internal backup for critical staff positions. This usually means you need

For most mission critical positions that require immediate expertise, hire the experience! Annotations: 12, Page 154 – Suggestions On Building an Internal Staff.

a training program that will allow newer people to develop the skills that will enable them to increase their value to your organization.

FOR EFFECTIVE LEASING, USE ONLY A SELF-MANAGED IN-HOUSE LEASING AGENT. I think the delegation of leasing to an outside source is a very risky business. Leasing agents usually have other projects they are trying to fill. How do you know they are not taking prospects from your project to another one? The biggest problem, especially in retail leasing, is filling up the last 20 percent of a project. Leasing brokers typically stall on the last phase of leasing since most of the commissions are earned filling up the easier and larger spaces. With an internal leasing staff you can manage the whole leasing process much better and avoid the inherent problems of third party leasing agents.

John has made a good case for an in-house leasing staff. If, however, you are buying or developing your first project and it is not large enough to justify putting in place an in-house staff, you should consider using the services of an outside leasing agent. See Annotation: 10, Page 150 – An In-house Property Management & Leasing Organization and Annotation: 35, Page 196 – Retail Property Leasing Recommendations.

YOU SHOULD HAVE STANDARDIZED AGREEMENTS IN PLACE FOR ALL ASPECTS OF CONDUCTING YOUR BUSINESS which include leasing, employment, accounting procedures, company benefits, and compensation.

After you develop a winning investment formula, stick with it. This doesn't mean you shouldn't try new ventures. Just make sure that the new venture does not put your already successful business plan at risk.

> An attorney should be part of your team for reviewing employment agreements and all leasing contracts. Annotations: 50, Page 214 – An Attorney Should be Part of Your Team.

INCREASE AND CONTINUALLY SHOP FOR COMPETITIVE LENDERS AND LARGER CREDIT LINES. Develop and maintain financial relationships with local lenders. Almost anyone starting or evolving in the real estate business is using leverage to build their portfolio. It is very risky if you limit your borrowings to one lender without building other relationships. In spite of promises to the contrary, there is no lender that I know of that is in the market all the time. If you only have one or two lender relationships, your ability to financially manage your portfolio will always be at a higher risk. I have found that local lenders

> Construction and development loans on shopping centers are usually subject to personal liability: the lender can go after the borrowers personal assets in a default. Annotations: 49, Page 213 – Construction and Development Loans for Retail Projects.

should be on your list of contacts since they will make more aggressive loans because of their greater familiarity with the market.

 Tenant relations is one of the critical roles that should be given to only the most competent people on your staff.

Make every effort to minimize tenant turnover unless upgrading. Tenant relations is one of the critical roles that should be given to only the most competent people on your staff. A favorable tenant experience will make it easier on re-leasing. More importantly, if the tenant needs additional locations, they will turn to you for the new space. There are many successful developers who have grown significant empires by expanding as a result of their tenants' need for additional space.

Current Observations

The importance of the role John Hamilton's parents took in his life is evidenced by the place of honor their portrait occupies in his Houston office. Having commissioned an artist to do the portrait based on an old photograph, John's parents bear witness to the fruits of their son's labors as the founder of one of the most successful development operations in Houston.

John's primary business, Option 1 Realty Group, focuses on large and small retail strip centers. The firm is also moving into the luxury condominium market, particularly in resort areas.

With a $200 million asset base and a portfolio structured for minimal risk, John doesn't have to worry very much about the return of the plastic spoon. He owns a private jet and collects Harley-Davidsons and rare political history memorabilia. He also makes sure his wife and six children have the kind of life he wasn't able to enjoy as a child. And he does it all under the watchful gaze of his parents, who would be very pleased to see that the house their son built is doing so well.

Further Reading

See the following Annotations on other topics relating to retail investment real estate:

Annotations: 40, Page 203 - Important Retail Lease Provisions.
Annotations: 42, Page 206 - Parking.

Chapter Four

Gerald Marcil

"I never thought I would be married to real estate—I thought it was just something I would get out of my system."

I INVEST IN APARTMENTS IN AREAS BETWEEN THE BEST AND THE WORST.

In these cusp areas you typically get to choose from an array of fixer-uppers in better areas.

ACHIEVEMENT HIGHLIGHTS

- Earned real estate license in college

- Worked his way through school

- Returned to real estate after college

- Successful single-family home broker

- Graduated to apartment investing

- Developed a successful formula

- Learned lessons in real estate crash

- Current portfolio above $150 million

On Early Beginnings

I grew up the son of a North Dakota farmer. My father told me that I should feel lucky because all my needs were covered—I had food and shelter. I appreciated what was provided but I also had a strong desire to accomplish more. At the time I wasn't sure quite how to proceed, but I knew that I needed to find a path to greater happiness.

After graduating from high school I headed off to southern California for college. I worked my way through school as a part time machinist and house painter. While I was working for minimum wage trying to put myself through school, one of my friends got a real estate license. I watched him start to make what I considered serious money buying and selling property.

At 20, I got my own real estate license and tried my hand at sales, concentrating on the single-family home market. I did not do as well as I had hoped as a part time real estate broker and assumed that the real estate brokerage business was not for me.

I assumed that the real estate brokerage business was not for me.

I graduated from the University of Southern California with the goal of opening a bar and restaurant. A friend of mine who was to be my partner in the bar business was holding things up, so in the interim I embarked on a road trip to the East Coast and back.

I never thought I would be married to real estate—I thought it was just something I would get out of my system. But I had an epiphany while I was traveling across the country. I realized I did not want to be in the bar or restaurant business, nor did I want to interview with large corporations and end up wearing a necktie for thirty years. When I looked at the opportunities available for an aspiring recent college graduate and compared those opportunities to their respective risk, I kept on going back to the real estate business.

On a Full Time Commitment to Real Estate

So I went back to brokering single family homes and was rewarded by making six sales in my first month back. As opposed to my part time college effort, I was really committed and focused on the job and it showed. Six sales in the first month? Even I was surprised. Then I made two more sales the next month. The market was just heating up and that helped, so my timing was good.

In that short time, I made $8,500 in commissions, compared to $8,000 I made in a year as a machinist.

In my first year as a real estate broker, I made $90,000. During that period, I was being mentored by another broker who told me the real money was in rental property. In spite of my success, I wanted to get out of single-family housing sales. People's emotions were getting to me and I didn't want to deal with color and kitchen cabinet choices.

On Entry to Investment Property Ownership

I started getting into brokering duplexes and four-plexes and liked that better. I was involved with lawyers, accountants and business people, and had lots of fun working with professionals. By getting familiar with things like arcane tax laws, exchange procedures, property management, and complicated financing, I made more sales. In the process of working smaller income property deals, I found an apartment investment opportunity and bought it with another investor. I went in for 25 percent; my partner put up the balance.

I continued investing and also tried my hand at managing apartments for both my account and other investors. By 1980 I had 72 units that I was managing. When I looked at where I was spending my time and compared it to where I was making my money, I came to the realization that I was spending too much time managing. I hired a University of Southern California

> I had about 72 units I was managing and came to the realization I was spending too much time managing.

alum to run my real estate management firm. This let me get back into sales and investing on a full time basis, although I still had to devote some time making sure the property management operation was working effectively.

 An annual line-item budget for income and expenses must be established between the off-site management team and the owner. Annotations: 11, Page 152 - Suggestions on Working with Off-Site Managers (Internal or Third Party).

I started putting my money into cusp areas. I was usually the largest investor in these real estate partnerships—the other 75 percent might be spread out over 10 people. I made a fee and I got a percentage of the profit. The deals got bigger and bigger—from 9 units to 15 to 25 units and up.

On Developing Real Estate Investment Strategies

I am a believer in investing in apartments in areas between the best and the worst. I call these cusp areas. I conduct extensive research to identify such areas where I feel the risk and opportunity offer a good mix between potential increases in cash flow, appreciation, and future marketability.

It doesn't make sense to me to buy a fixer-upper in a blighted area or a low-rent district. It doesn't matter what you do to it—it is very difficult and risky to make money compared to investing in cusp areas. There are investors who specialize in higher-risk areas, but their goal is to survive rental collection and hopefully benefit from what could be high cash flow. Also, when those properties go up for sale, there are a very limited number of buyers who are willing to take higher risks, and most of them are looking for the same thing— low price and high cash flow. That combined with the difficulty in financing such projects completes the circle of undesirability.

But cusp areas are different. You typically get to choose from an array of fixer-uppers in much better areas. The money you invest there if prudently spent can result in a better product commanding higher rents. Good management can make those buildings very rewarding. As a result of being in better areas you usually get a much better cross section of good tenants to choose from. If you fix a building up, you can continue to get good tenants which can add to the appeal, manageability, and income potential of the project.

It helps if you're an active rather than passive investor, because if you're passive, it's just not worth it, even in the cusp areas. You have to be on top of the market, be willing to make changes and that means you have to be local and on site.

You have to be on top of the market, be willing to make changes, and that means you have to be local and on site.

On Surviving a Market Cycle

As my portfolio grew and as the market for fixer uppers became inundated with buyers, I got away from rehabilitating properties and bought buildings that were under construction. That was when the market was at the top of its cycle, in 1989.

With Détente, the end of the first Gulf War, and the collapse of southern California's defense-related job market, investor demand and rents for all types of investment real estate suffered dramatically. The early 1990s brought with it the rolling real estate recession that had afflicted many other parts of the country in the mid- to late 1980s. After losing a significant number of aerospace jobs in So. Calif., and the resulting loss of jobs in other industries, a depression-like atmosphere settled into the southern California real estate market.

> Los Angeles had a net loss of 107,000 jobs from 2001 to 2003, mainly in manufacturing, business services, trade, transportation, and warehousing. Annotations: 53, Page 217 - Job Loss in Los Angeles County.

The combination of job loss, rising interest rates, and declining rents made the early 1990s the Grim Reaper for those who owned highly-leveraged real estate. Those owners who found themselves in that situation were usually the ones who lost their buildings, their equity, their confidence, and in some extreme cases, their financial lives.

I worked hard, went into an intensive management

mode and kept my credit clean so I could jump when things got better in the mid-1990s. I also had the benefit of avoiding the double-edged sword of excessive leverage as a result of my more conservative approach to financing.

On Riding an Up Market and Evaluating Risk

The market continued to be weak until 1994 and 1995. When the market turned, I was ready.

Some good advice for a real estate investor is to maintain a positive attitude through the experience of a negative result. You could have a lot of dry wells before you get a gusher. It takes a certain type of personality to deal with failure. Real estate is a risk taker's industry and if you don't have that mentality, you are going to have problems.

New real estate investors should take greater risks. Your tolerance for risk is usually influenced by your cycle in life. As an investor matures and their portfolio grows, the desire to take on more risk typically reduces. As a new, young investor you should not be as concerned with risk, as long as you have some buffer between your ambitions and reality.

> **Real estate is a risk taker's industry and if you don't have that mentality, you are going to have problems.**

Leverage permitted by lenders is influenced by the relationship between loan amount and market value and the relationship between annual debt payments and the property income. Annotations: 17 Page 163 – Leverage and Financing Investments.

YOU SHOULD USE AS MUCH LEVERAGE AS YOU CAN IN THE BEGINNING. Lenders are more sophisticated today, so they will act as a brake that will help to keep you from careening into trouble.

🦐 Advice to New Investors

Back when I started I didn't have patience. Patience, discipline, and research are critical to investing in income-producing real estate. After you develop your basic investment strategy, you need the discipline and patience to reach your goals. Even the greatest amount of research will get you only so far.

There will be setbacks, so you have to anticipate them as best as possible and not give up on executing your business plan. I had to learn the hard way that you can't overextend financially and you cannot quit.

You also have to be willing to roll up your sleeves, get involved with your properties, and work hard. It was easy for me because I had nothing to lose. When I got into real estate I had $2,000 which I spent on an old BMW. I also had one suit. Since I really had nothing, failure was not an option for me.

I think another big key to my investing success is thinking strategically, thinking visually. I would often ask: where are the jobs? Is the job market going up or down? So I only wanted to invest in developed areas.

 Stronger markets can be identified by above average job growth, low housing affordability, and above average apartment occupancies. Annotations: 24, Page 176 - Analyzing Apartment Markets. Annotations: 25, Page 178 - Stronger Markets Can Be Identified By.

On Market Timing

I don't know when the market will peak or when it will bottom out. I stay in it at all times and just try to buy the best deals at any given time. My strategy is buy high, low, and in the middle. It will average out over the long haul. I have only seen income property come down twice in 30 years (1981-1982 and 1991-1994). How can I predict five years out of 30?

On Negotiating Deals and Reputation

I perform on the deals I get into. If I open escrow, I close. I have a reputation for not wasting people's time and not nit picking the inspections or asking the seller to fix a lot of little things. I also have a reputation for handling difficult deals—ones where there might be environmental issues about title, zoning, earthquake damage, termite damage, asbestos, difficult tenants, extreme deferred maintenance, etc.

I never demean the seller's property. I let them know I love it. No one wants to sell to someone who doesn't like their property. It can help me get a better price, because my interest often makes the seller more willing to accept a lower offer.

> The negotiating process should be approached from the perspective of your long-term goals against the backdrop of current market conditions.
> Annotations: 56, Page 220 - Negotiating Investment Real Estate Transactions.

Very rarely do I try to re-trade or renegotiate a property after we reach initial agreement. It only happens when something huge turns up during due diligence and I still want the property.

I don't like auctions or bidding situations. I only do it when I really like the property and I think I see some potential in it that no one else does.

Know your bottom line. Don't get emotional.

On Working With Brokers

I like working with brokers. I speak their lingo because I was a broker, and I have kept my broker's license active. It's important to find brokers who are sophisticated and won't waste my time.

Agents like to work with me because they know I am fair with them. They bring me their deals first. I don't work with a lot of agents, which makes the ones I do work with feel special and which also breeds loyalty. I learned how to treat an agent when I used to make a living as one.

Active local brokers can be found on www.loopnet.com by checking brokers who have the most listings in the target area; CoStar (www.costar.com) is a fee service with extensive data on broker activity; local title companies that handle commercial transactions; local commercial real estate appraisers and attorneys that specialize in real estate law. Annotations: 4, Page 135 – Selecting the Right Broker.

 ## On Inspections and Due Diligence

I do most of the important due diligence myself, but I have a staff or hire someone to inspect all of the apartments, read all of the title reports, study all of the leases and other tedious tasks.

Due Diligence Checklist.
Annotations 63, Page 230.

Adjustments to Rents for Amenities. Annotations 64, Page 243.

Careful due diligence that can reveal pumped-up rents includes examining the last 12 months operating records, rental records, questioning the resident manager about recent changes in rental policy, examination of miscellaneous expenses, and a unit-by-unit comparison of rents and occupancy levels. Annotations: 18, Page 168 – Identifying Apartment Projects That Have Been "Hot-Rodded" For Sale.

My inspection and due diligence checklists are extensive. I do rent comparisons, and determine whether it fits my strategy in terms of size, age, unit types, what kind of tenants live there and what direction is the area going. I inspect all units, title reports, leases, large maintenance items and environmental reports.

I also think it's a good idea to look out for buildings that have been "hot-rodded" for sale, which means the rents are too high to maintain due to recent large scale rent increases. Don't get blinded by a fresh coat of paint—there still may be a lot of deferred maintenance.

Look out for buildings that have been "hot-rodded" for sale.

On Hints For Rehabbing

When I tour the properties I look for opportunities to improve them which should result in the ability to charge higher rents. I have found that, as long as the rent increase will pay for the rehab over the expected life of the rehab, it's worth doing. Every dollar of rehab should raise the value and tenant quality.

There should be multiple factors between rehab costs, rental increases, and resulting building value. A dollar of rehab should equate to an increase in rent, which in turn should increase your value by three to five times, sometimes more than the cost of the rehab. We also discount the value of the rent increase to cover net present value of rehab over its life at the current Cap Rate for the market as a

Rehabs should not be attempted unless occupancy and rents can be increased as a result. Exceptions include health and safety expenditures and cosmetic improvements to keep the structure esthetically competitive. Maximizing curb appeal should be a high priority for attracting and keeping a better quality of tenant. Annotations: 19, Page 170 – Apartment Rehab Costs and Payback Formulas.

A capitalization rate or CAP rate is a ratio used to estimate the value of income producing properties. A CAP rate is derived by taking the net operating income of a property divided by the sales price or value of a property expressed as a percentage. Annotations: 57, Page 223 - Capitalization Rates.

test to see if the rehab makes sense.

For the rehab process, I get three bids from people who can (and will) perform the work. Typically we go with the low bid, but if bids are close, we go with the guy we have had a good experience with.

We have some of our own guys to do this—but typically we use third parties.

On Portfolio Management

I am continually asking myself the question of where I can do better with my equity without dramatically changing my risk. I don't like to sell or trade. I prefer to refinance and use that money. I will also continually reinvest money from the sale of development projects. I will sell or trade when I don't have the money to complete an acquisition or if I need cash for a larger development.

If I don't need the cash I would rather do a tax deferred exchange rather than sell. My first question is, "Am I getting a good deal on my up-leg property?" Investors who continually work building their real estate portfolios reap certain benefits, but also could be faced with more risk

> **Tax deferred exchanges** are used by many investors to increase the rate at which they build their real estate portfolios. This is possible as a result of being able to postpone taxes on sale. Annotations: 60, Page 225 – Tax Deferred Exchanges.

and complications in their exit strategy.

Selling should be a last resort and will be influenced by the after-tax proceeds. With current capital gains rates relatively low, the tax on sale is low, which means selling and paying taxes makes more sense today.

On Development

In the early 1980s, I built a townhouse project from scratch. There was a lot of luck involved. You can come into times where interest rates are high and tenant or investor demand is low. I did lose money on my first 18-unit townhouse project. It was a valuable lesson because I realized that during certain cycles, the market dictated how much money I made and the options were all bad. The experience was humbling, but a relatively cheap lesson, although I didn't think so at the time. Learn this: if you are developing and the market is bad, you are not going to make money in the short term. Your only hope is that somehow you have a way to financially survive until the cycle changes.

If you are developing and the market is bad, you are not going to make money in the short term.

In keeping with my philosophy of patience, I waited for the cycle to change. As a result, my recent development efforts have been very profitable. The change was that I had the benefit of many more years

Before entering into a "battle of building permits," a developer should investigate a city's political attitude towards development. Even if the environment is welcoming, there are many steps before the start of construction. Annotations: 7, Page 144 – The Politics of Developing.

The Endangered Species Act has opened the door to a new set of challenges for developers. Annotation: 8, Page 146 – Miscellaneous Development Risks.

of experience, much deeper pockets, and an eight to ten year up market in terms of appreciating real estate. The degree of importance is not necessarily in the correct order.

I only recommend development to those willing to take much more risk of somehow missing a down cycle. The biggest risk is that most loans carry personal liability. This factor alone was the noose that hung countless developers with Trump-like dreams and Mickey Mouse balance sheets.

On Current Portfolio Status and Strategy

All of my properties are in California in Los Angeles and Orange counties. There are 11 apartment building properties consisting of 817 units. There are seven development properties consisting of 830 units.

I do more development projects now, and I don't leverage the apartment buildings as much.

Summary Advice For New Investors

My advice to new real estate investors is to have patience. Take the long view. You can leverage in the beginning if you don't have much money. As you get more property, lower the leverage so you can weather the storms. Don't be afraid to move forward in any market—only be afraid of over-leveraging. If you have time, buy fixers in cusp areas and fix them up. Go with only the best agents.

Over-confidence should be avoided. Always weigh your downside, but when the odds are in your favor, don't be afraid to bet. Avoid trying to make a living by predicting or out-negotiating the next guy. Implement strong and basic management practices that allow the client (the renter or buyer) to get more than what they are paying for. Always be honest. Never think it will be easy.

Always weigh your downside, but when the odds are in your favor, don't be afraid to bet.

You need a certain personality to succeed in real estate. I see smart people who don't make it because analysis paralyzes them and they don't take risks. Then

I see fewer smart people who take risks and succeed. You're not going to make money in real estate if you spend all your time analyzing things. That's a real estate investor's biggest downfall.

Taking on partners helps smaller investors share in economies of scale, benefit from the experience of the sponsor, and compete for larger deals. Questions are: who puts up the money, what are the fees to the sponsor, and how are the cash flow and proceeds from a sale distributed? Annotations: 5, Page 139 – Real Estate Partnerships – Sponsor vs. Investor. Who Gets What?

People are more sophisticated than they used to be. Contracts are 12 pages instead of two. It's a much more litigious society. Fewer people take responsibility for themselves, and more people like to play victim. We're being sued now for things that have always been here, like mold.

When you start out you have to be more creative. Borrow money, or get a group of partners together for a deal. It isn't easy. Your goal should be to not need partners but in growing a business the ability to raise equity from third party investors could give you an edge over poorly capitalized investors. In the beginning, I always felt better with partners because I didn't need as much leverage to close some of my earlier deals.

If you're new to real estate, you have to learn financing in order to understand a good deal. If you buy the property right, you can work with banks and lenders to get financing. There is some leverage involved, but if you have the right deal then the money will be easy to find. Otherwise, lenders will consider you a dreamer who chases down unrealistic deals. So the lender must know that you have a working knowledge of market pricing. You might have some administrative loopholes to conquer, but it will work.

The more confidently you know your market, the better you'll be able to spot a good deal. Remember that it's a supply and demand market. If you know what the true value of a property is and project

The more confidently you know your market, the better you'll be able to spot a good deal.

an air of confidence to lenders and bankers, they'll see that you are knowledgeable and will feel more comfortable helping you.

Can you be a successful part-time real estate investor? Possibly. I have seen people do quite well and establish great retirement funds as part time real estate investors. That said, to succeed you have to partner with someone who is full-time. Find someone you trust to be there full-time.

Be sure you know the market and the trends. You have to act like an appraiser and know the current market value.

Personal Thoughts

I don't believe in winning through intimidation, but I liked the ice ball theory in the book *Winning Through Intimidation*—the earth will burn out in six million years so nothing is really a big deal.

I can only be secure in myself. No amount of material wealth will make me secure. The only things that really count are my friends and family—and my relationship with the creator.

Real estate investing is no easy ride in spite of my somewhat oversimplified and abbreviated comments. There are many astute people who get on the real estate investment wave only to get soaked, and some drown. You have to be willing to roll up your sleeves, get involved with your properties and work hard.

I am not the first to realize that this is not an easy business. But as my father always said, "**IF IT WAS PROFITABLE AND EASY, EVERYBODY WOULD DO IT.**"

Further Reading

See the following Annotations on other topics relating to investing and managing apartments:

Annotations: 21, Page 173 - Professional Apartment Management.

Annotations: 62, Page 229 - Unsolicited Offers.

The Foundations of Their Wealth

MARCEL ARSENAULT

"Location is important, but not as significant as having the right people assist you in determining the correct strategy that contributes to current and future cash flow."

"The key is not projecting the problems of the past but looking at the future and how cash flow can be increased."

BEN LEEDS

"When buyers disappear and cash flows erode, the market can change to the negative quickly."

"Management is an evolving process. Personnel changes should be thought through. Compromise in key positions will almost always lead to trouble."

"If an investor can increase cash flow beyond what the existing owner has been able to generate, the opportunity for appreciation can be multiplied exponentially."

In Their Own Words

JOHN HAMILTON

"After you develop a winning investment formula, stick with it. Make sure the new venture does not put your already successful business plan at risk."

"Increase and continually shop for competitive lenders and larger credit lines. It is risky to limit your borrowings to one lender."

"Secondary locations are tempting because of the lower cost of the land. The problem is the land is at a lower price for a reason."

GERALD MARCIL

"I am continually asking myself where I can do better with my equity without dramatically changing my risk."

"As a new, young investor you should not be as concerned with risk if you have some buffer between your ambitions and reality."

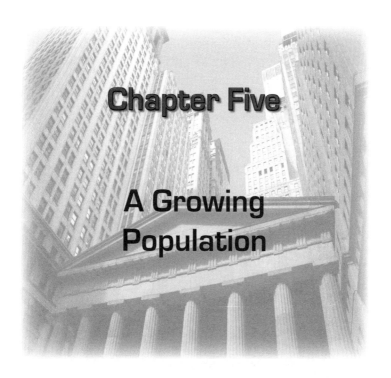

Chapter Five

A Growing Population

It's no secret that privately-held real estate is a comparatively scarce asset in the United States.

A Favorable Long-Term Outlook for Real Estate

*E*ighty percent of the land mass of the nation is held either by the Government or is in agricultural use. That leaves only one-fifth of the area to support all commercial and residential uses, including the infrastructure that is the backbone of commerce. The population density of the U.S. in 2005 is approximately 80 persons per square mile, but effectively (adjusting for the Government and farming sectors) we are supporting 400 persons per square mile for most of our improved land uses. Between 2005 and 2020, Census projections show an increase of more than

As intensity of land use increases, the upward pressure on real estate values is a persistent feature of the national economy.

40 million Americans, which will bring effective population density above 450 persons per square mile. The 2000 Census indicated that 79 percent of the U.S. population is concentrated in urban areas, a proportion

that continues to increase over time. As intensity of land use increases, the upward pressure on real estate values is a persistent feature of the national economy.

Anticipating the impact of demographic change on real estate demand is aided by an examination of the "population pyramid," or the array of total population by its age/sex distribution. Here are the pyramids for 2000 and 2020.

U.S. Census Bureau Population Pyramids by Age Group

2000

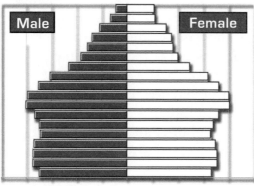

2020 Projected

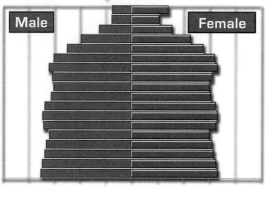

Residential/Multifamily

The rise in the U.S. homeownership rate during the past decade has undoubtedly been accelerated by low mortgage interest rates, especially since the Fed's aggressive moves to cut rates in 2002. However, the demographics tell us that this period was exactly the time when the Baby Boom generation was in its economic prime, with the bulge in population between 40 and 54 years of age, when earnings are at or near their peak and families are being raised. By 2020, however, this generation shifts into another phase of life as empty-nesters and active retirees. Most observers expect housing preferences to shift from the single-family home—often suburban—to some form of multi-housing, either rental or condominium, more appropriate to smaller household size and with less individual maintenance responsibility. Interestingly, this is expected to benefit both moderate density Sunbelt locations (either as retirement or second homes) and higher-density cities with strong entertainment and cultural attractions.

> **Most observers expect housing preferences to shift from the single-family home to some form of multi-housing.**

Simultaneously, the young-earners cohort, from 25 to 34 years, will be growing from about 39 million (the baby bust) to 45 million (the echo boom), adding to the pool of potential apartment renters as it goes through the early career and family formation phase of life. A third component of housing demand stems from immigration, which accounts for about 40 percent of U.S. population growth. Most immigrants are of working age when they arrive in the U.S. Although most assimilate into the mainstream, and ultimately become homeowners, the great majority are renters during their first decade in the country. Taken together, trends indicate that about 5.3 million rental units will be needed to simply accommodate population growth through 2020, without accounting for the need to replace outmoded or substandard housing.

Industrial

THE FORCES OF GLOBALIZATION AND THE HIGH CONSUMPTION PROPENSITY OF THE U.S. POPULATION IS EXPECTED TO INCREASE DEMAND FOR WAREHOUSE/DISTRIBUTION SPACE THROUGH 2020. Gateway cities and regional distribution hubs in particular will need to add capacity in the decade or more ahead. The maps on the following pages illustrate the projected rise in truck freight, as anticipated by the Federal Highway Administration.

The existing base of industrial space, already tallied at more than 12 billion square feet by the Society of Industrial and Office Realtors (SIOR), will need to expand substantially to handle the increased volume of goods moving through the logistics network.

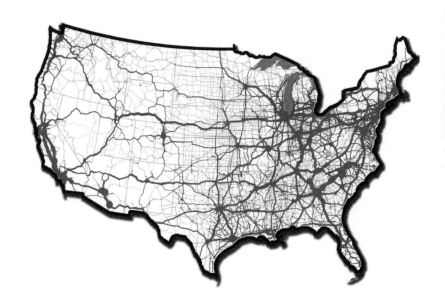

Estimated Average
Daily Truck Traffic: 1998

TRUCK VOLUME SCALE

| 50,000 | 25,000 | 12,500 |

US Dept. of Transportation
Federal Highway Administration
Office of Freight Management and Operations
Freight Analysis Framework

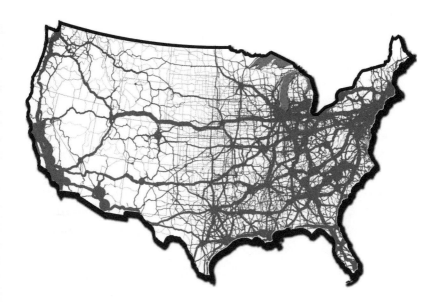

Estimated Average
Daily Truck Traffic: 2020

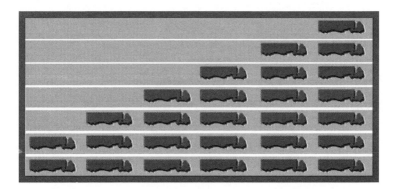

The maps indicate that the Northeast corridor from Boston to Washington will see especially intense activity, as will California from San Diego northward through the Central Valley up to the Bay Area. NAFTA trade effects are apparent in markets proximate to Mexico and along the Canadian border from Buffalo to Detroit. Meanwhile, freight flows will be accelerating along most of the Interstate routes east of the Mississippi, particularly along the Charlotte-Atlanta axis, and in the Midwest network centered on Chicago, radiating into the mid-South and west on I-80. A recent Brookings Institution study (Toward a New Metropolis: The Opportunity to Rebuild America) makes a rough estimate of an additional billion square feet of industrial space to be needed over the coming decades, a net increase that must also account for the significant replacement in many markets of obsolete lofts, warehouses, and light manufacturing buildings.

An additional billion square feet of industrial space will be needed over the coming decades.

 Office

Reflecting the secular change in America's industry structure, services-producing industries are projected to account for the vast majority of the 33 million jobs that will be added to the U.S. economy through 2020. Although many of those jobs will fall outside the office sector (in education, health, and social services, for example), some of the fastest-growing job categories will in office-intensive sectors such as professional and business services, finance, and information, according to projections from the U.S. Department of Labor.

> Fastest-growing job categories will be office-intensive such as professional and business services, finance, and information.

SIOR's 2005 Comparative Statistics volume indicates more than four billion square feet of office space in the country, with an occupancy rate of about 85 percent. If office employment grows at the expected 2.5 percent annual rate through 2020, the nation will need a net increase in office inventory of one billion square feet to sustain a 90 percent occupancy rate. Construction will actually need to be somewhat higher than this to account for replacement and conversion of space, since in many markets older office buildings are being taken out of service either by demolition or by adaptive re-use.

Projections from the Brookings Institution study, Toward a New Metropolis, identify a series of Sunbelt markets extending from South Florida to Southern California—led by Las Vegas, Austin, and Phoenix— as the fastest growing markets in terms of expected office construction. But it would be a mistake to count out the big cities, as the absolute volume of space required will be greatest in New York City, Los Angeles, Washington, Chicago, San Francisco, and Boston.

Retail

SHOPPING CENTERS ARE AN ESPECIALLY COMPLEX PROPERTY TYPE, since there are considerations of size (from the stand-alone store and "high-street" shop, though the neighborhood or strip center, up to the super-regional mall) which stratify the market, as well as considerations of function or target segment—the traditional mall, the big-box center, the lifestyle center, etc. The retail property industry is constantly evolving, and the only thing to be said with certainty is that it will innovate further through 2020.

The outlook for retail properties, though, is inextricably bound up with household growth and household spending patterns. As such, it most often follows a "rooftops" strategy, aiming at the development of new centers in proximity to fast-growing and affluent communities. Thus we should see the continuation of perimeter-related expansion such as we have seen in places like Frisco, Texas, north of Dallas, and in Orange County, N.Y., 60 miles or so north of Manhattan. But retailers also have noted that urban "infill" retailing can be an effective strategy, particularly in the so-called 24-hour cities where very high sales per square foot are achievable.

For many shopping center investors, too, there will be a key distinction between store-types that are inextricably tied to sheer head-count, such as supermarket and most mass-market apparel outlets, and those serving higher disposable income consumers, including specialty foods, electronics, and high-fashion apparel. And, although Internet shopping has not proven an across-the-board threat to retail property, as some feared in the late 1990s, certain segments like music, books, and sporting goods are seeing slow growth as consumers use the World Wide Web to hunt for the widest choice and best bargains in these categories.

Segments like music, books, and sporting goods are seeing slow growth as consumers use the World Wide Web.

 **Hotels**

Like retail centers, hotels are a highly segmented and specialized property type where generalizations are difficult to sustain. It is safe to say, however, that a well-diversified hotel market is supported by three principal travel sources: business travelers, international visitors, and domestic vacationers. Air travel is by far the best indicator of overnight trip trends in the public data, and in 2003 there were nearly 600 million enplanements at U.S. airports, up 27.4 percent from ten years earlier. After the horrendous experience of 9/11/2001, air travel has been rebuilding its volume, as has hotel occupancy. Estimates of additional capacity needs for major airports is therefore quite pertinent to expected growth in hotel demand.

> **By 2013, the FAA believes that the three key airports serving New York all will require extra capacity.**

By 2013, the FAA believes that the three key airports serving New York—LaGuardia, JFK, and Newark-Liberty—all require extra capacity. Philadelphia, now booming because of the entry of Southwest Airlines to its roster, is also straining with its load. O'Hare in Chicago is on the list, as are the two South Florida facilities in Ft. Lauderdale and Palm Beach, although both have been substantially expanded and upgraded in the recent past. Four California facilities are identified: John Wayne/Orange County, Burbank and Long Beach near Los Angeles, and Oakland International.

San Antonio and Houston/Hobby in Texas, Tucson, and Albuquerque round out the list. Several of those airports remain on the agency's growth chart for 2020 (see the map below), and are joined by Islip/Long Island, Bradley International in Connecticut (serving Hartford and Springfield, MA), Providence, Chicago/Midway, Atlanta/Hartsfield, Birmingham, Las Vegas/McCarren, and Ontario in California's Inland Empire.

The outlook for the long term in the hospitality industry must start with the recognition that it is only now that hotels are getting past the trough of the early 2000s recession and the terrorism-induced travel collapse. By 2006–2007, the industry expects to be back on track in providing very attractive investment yields. Thereafter, it is a question of managing the tricky supply/demand equation in an industry where real estate is rented by the night. Defending and enhancing brand names, finding opportunities in secondary markets under the radar screen, creating a distinctive non-commodity hotel experience appropriate to market location and price niche, and keeping a fine eye on costs are all on the menu for hotel owners and managers.

> **By 2006–2007, the industry expects to be back on track in providing very attractive investment yields.**

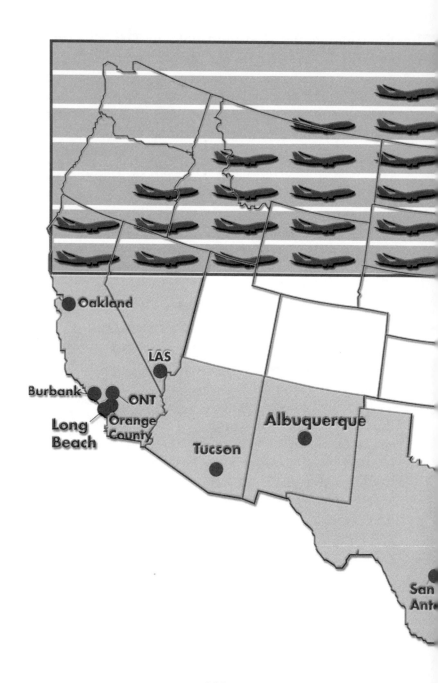

Airports and Metro Areas the FAA Predicts Will Need Additional Capacity by 2020

 All Property Types

For all property types, the future will surely hold at least one full economic and market cycle of peak/recession/recovery during the 2005-2020 period—and probably more than one. There is no credible way to estimate the timing other than to say that in early 2005 the near-term outlook is for several years of growth. The important strategic perspective is that the inevitable cycles are fluctuations in a longer-term trend of growth.

Most real estate professionals concur that job generation is the single most important economic indicator for fundamental commercial real estate demand. It is therefore instructive to recall, as displayed in the following graph, how wrinkles in the job chart predictably return to the long-range growth rate. Rooted in demography, the need for real estate can only increase when positive population and employment change is measured in the tens of millions of persons.

Post-Recession Employment Plateaus Give Way to Extended Gains

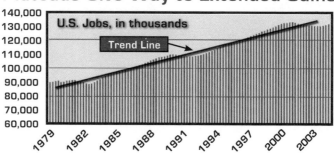

Investment Capital: A Deep and Diverse Pool

Estimates of the capital value of commercial real estate, inclusive of multi-family assets, now approach the $5 trillion mark, counting both debt and equity investment. Hard lessons were learned during the industry's liquidity crisis from 1989 to 1992, but those lessons led to structural changes in the way real estate capital is accessed and deployed. It was encouraging to see how quickly the industry responded, in a disciplined way, to the sudden curtailment in the economy in 2001, restraining development and tightening underwriting for commercial property debt. But even more impressive was the industry's ability to discern the differences in the 2000's cycle when compared to the event of a decade before, and adjust capital flows and pricing without resorting to a shut-down that would have driven values down precipitously. This was the sign of a more mature, more sophisticated market, with a more powerful panoply of tools to manage its investment environment.

Although the industry and general business press are captivated by headline deals, the remarkable fact is that nearly one-half of real estate's total capitalization comes from non-institutional sources. This is a broad pool of private investment—private individuals, family trusts, small

Nearly one-half of real estate's total capitalization comes from non-institutional sources.

investment partnerships and LLCs, entrepreneurial business—that together account for well over two and a quarter trillion dollars, according to the 2005 Emerging Trends in Real Estate.

Whereas in the 1980s much of the pool of private capital was assembled by tax-motivated syndications with an appetite for generating losses as offsets to ordinary income, the contemporary investor has economic incentives aligned with performance—positive cash flow and property value appreciation. This is not to say that taxes no longer matter. They clearly do, and the tax-advantaged position of real estate clearly motivates many if not all non-institutional investors. The ability to take depreciation of property improvements, and to deduct mortgage interest expense, enhances after-tax cash flow at the property level and provides yields that are difficult to match in other investment asset classes.

Sensitivity to demographics helps us in teasing out another part of private investors' motivations. As the Baby Boom generation is squarely in its pre-retirement period, many of them are heeding the counsel of financial advisors to shift from an emphasis on stocks, which are appreciation oriented but volatile in price, and adopt a capital conservation strategy that looks to narrower price swings and a higher income component for total yield. In an earlier era, they might have recommended fixed income investments, but good quality bonds provide very low coupon rates, and their value is subject to discounting when, as is virtually certain, interest rates rise from their recent low levels. With the availability of favorable leverage from low-cost mortgages, private investors have been able to realize double-digit returns and comfortable cushions against risk even with overall capitalization rates at the low end of their historical range. Although there is some hint of speculative fever among small investors in some markets, by and large the growth in the volume of non-institutional investment should continue as Boomers move larger percentages of their wealth into property for its combination of income yields, tax-shelter, and comparatively low volatility.

Growth in non-institutional investment should continue as Boomers move larger percentages of their wealth into property.

Pension funds themselves are in the process of formally raising their asset allocations to real estate. And, in the enormous U.S. pension fund industry, now with about $6.5 trillion in total assets, a small shift in asset allocation can mean a huge increase in the funds available to real estate. The critical element in watching such a shift is that the funds, once having moved to a higher allocation, have done so for strategic reasons and are unlikely to reverse course suddenly.

What the pension funds have learned in the more than a quarter-century of active investment in real estate is that commercial property has in fact delivered the diversification benefit it was expected to bring to mixed-asset portfolios. Real estate's cycle is not contemporary with stock market cycles, and so it serves as a valuable hedge in generating improved risk-adjusted returns to portfolio investors like the pension funds.

There is a place, now rigorously demonstrated, for real estate on the efficient frontier of portfolio yields.

There is a place, now rigorously demonstrated, for real estate on the efficient frontier of portfolio yields—that ideal curve where yield and risk are optimally priced. Each one percent movement upward in pension industry allocation means an additional $65 billion targeted toward real estate—and the pool of total pension fund assets grows each year, by nearly $600 billion from the fourth quarter 2003 to fourth quarter 2004. The amount represented by the NCREIF Index, $145 billion in 4,152 property investments as of the end of 2004, seems destined to expand dramatically over the coming decade.

Real estate investment trusts draw upon public capital markets, and have an even greater equity position than pension funds, with 153 equity REITs representing $261 billion in market capitalization as of early 2005. After a brief period during the 1990s when REITs positioned themselves as growth stocks —because of the steep discounts at which they were able to acquire distressed assets from the RTC and over-leveraged sponsors—the trusts have settled into a niche where they are viewed as high-dividend stocks like utilities, with the advantage of being tax-neutral at the level of the trust.

While the REITs are generally correlated with the broader stock market, they do avoid the burden of double taxation (at the corporate level, then again at the investor level). This efficiency is attractive to many investors. With more and more capital flowing into real estate-oriented mutual funds, the amount of money available through this source alone has risen to $45.8 billion.

The downward shift in the value of the dollar has made U.S. real estate acquisitions relatively cheap for off-shore investors. It is tempting to see this as the new hot money available to the industry, but in fact foreign investment in U.S. real estate normally looks beyond the currency-trading effect and expresses more fundamental investment motivations. There is an enormous amount of money seeking investment from abroad as a result of the negative trade balance of the United States—which represents positive capital flows for our trading partners, and which requires investment somewhere.

The downward shift in the value of the dollar has made U.S. real estate acquisitions relatively cheap for off-shore investors.

The second fundamental reason bringing real estate funds to the U.S. is the weak outlooks for several European nations and Japan, where an aging population has begun the process of workforce contraction—meaning a period of perhaps decades where some large industrialized economies will struggle to experience even moderate economic expansion. From that perspective, an economy like the U.S. where a growing workforce and increasing productivity forecasts long-run real GDP growth above two percent per year looks very good indeed.

An economy like the U.S. with long-run real GDP growth above two percent per year looks very good indeed.

The capital structure of the real estate industry is far more weighted to debt than to equity. There are an abundance of primary lenders, of course, including commercial banks, life insurance companies, and foreign investors. But the role of Commercial Mortgage-Back Securities can hardly be overestimated in safeguarding the essential liquidity of the industry. CMBS was one of the great innovations to come out of the savings and loan/RTC debacle, providing a secondary market for debt instruments structured in such a way that they can be rated like corporate bonds.

The CMBS structure has allowed the great majority of debt to trade as investment-grade securities, with appropriately thin spreads, while providing risk-seeking investors with high-yield paper. And, with the proceeds of CMBS issuance, the primary lenders are recapitalized for further mortgage originations and need not carry long-term mortgage on their balance sheets.

From a standing start, CMBS has grown to more than $400 billion in notes outstanding, and looks like it can sustain $75 billion or more in new issuance indefinitely into the future. The result is an ample quantity of reasonably priced commercial mortgages, the lubrication that real estate markets need for smooth functioning.

In terms of competing capital market instruments, real estate has rarely stood in a more favorable position. It served as a safety net for many investors when the "tech wreck" hit the stock market, and provided superior yields as interest rates plunged to the lowest levels in two generations. Despite undeniably rich pricing at present, real estate cap rates compare favorably to stock price/ earnings ratios that are still substantially higher than the long-term norm of 15 or so. Likewise, the stickiness of cap rates— their tendency to fluctuate

Despite rich pricing, real estate cap rates compare favorably to stock price/ earnings ratios.

within a narrow band—makes property attractive to income-oriented investors who are aware that fixed-income investments will deteriorate in price as coupon rates on bonds rise. Having performed well as investments during the past recession and the extended "jobless recovery," real estate now seems poised to improve occupancy and rental revenue in a period of general economic expansion.

It goes without saying that, all the positive fundamentals notwithstanding, risks must be taken into account. On the margin, there are high-leveraged deals with floating rate debt that will find themselves squeezed, especially if the Fed accelerates its round of tighter monetary policy unexpectedly.

In some hot markets there is trading speculation— that is, purchasing properties not for their real income potential, but in the expectation that they can be "flipped" as contracts, sometimes even before a building is completed! We are seeing a new cadre of inexperienced investors entering the market, too, as real estate investment becomes the next "in" thing.

But the biggest challenge is a very traditional one: investments are priced not upon past performance, but upon expectations of a future that is not guaranteed. **PLANNING FOR THE LONG-HAUL IS THE KEY TO SUCCESS IN REAL ESTATE, BECAUSE CYCLES ARE BUILT INTO THE MARKET.** Risk becomes excessive, and then the cycle exerts its corrective discipline. Then the mantra again comes to the lips of the industry, "Stay alive 'til ... " (any year ending in –5, it seems). Those who survive prosper in the next cycle. The biggest risk is to ignore risk. But with reasonable foresight and prudence, time is on the side of the real estate investment community through the year 2020. And probably beyond.

Annotations

65 Essentials

Taking on partners is one of the most common ways that smaller investors can compete for larger deals.

The fundamentals of real estate investment as practiced by our four success stories.

Annotations

What Factors Influence Change in the Value of Property?   1

There are four primary factors:

a) **The perception of the risk of collecting future income** is one factor. The most important aspect of this statement is the word perception. For instance, if a financially weak tenant occupies a building with a twenty year lease, the risk of collecting the future income could be significant. If it is perceived that the tenant's financial future is improving, as a result of being acquired by a much stronger competitor, the relative risk is less and the price of the real estate they occupy will go up (other things being equal).

b) **The assumed trend of the cash flow** is another factor. Anticipated increases in cash flow usually result in upward price pressure. If the immediate trend of cash flow has a slightly negative bias, it does not necessarily mean that the value is eroding. If it is presumed that in the near future cash flow will increase, it is probable that there will be upward pressure on the current price. It is important to note the difference between cash flow and net income. It is possible to have the net income from a property going up and the cash flow going down. Such a situation can occur with properties that are encumbered with variable rate loans. If the variable rate payments are increasing faster than the net income is increasing, cash flow will decrease, resulting in the downward pressure in the price of the property. If the loan can be paid off without significant penalty and/or costs, then the price erosion could be mitigated

c) **The relationship between the quantities of qualified buyers in the market compared to the number of properties available for sale** is the third factor. More buyers competing for a limited number of properties for sale usually drive prices up. The number of buyers for investment real estate is influenced by the availability of financing. As financing becomes more expensive and or restrictive, the population of buyers will decrease and prices typically follow.

d) **The yields on real estate compared to the yields on alternative investments such as stocks, bonds, mutual funds, money market funds,** etc., is the fourth factor. If the yield or return from competing investments goes down, the yield from real estate investments will have similar downward pressure resulting in an upward bias on real estate prices. Real estate has historically had yields higher than what has been perceived as more liquid investments such as stocks and bonds but the trend in relative pricing of investment real estate has followed the price and yield trends of other Wall Street investment options.

Market Shift Indicators   2

a) **For the casual investor, the earliest indicators of a market shift are difficult to ascertain.** There are four basic trends and another leading indicator that have to be monitored. The examples below are indicative of a market that is exhibiting early signs of a downward trend. The opposite effects would indicate a market that has an upward price bias.

i) The inventory of property for sale expands and remains on the market for greater periods of time.

ii) Transactions that are under contingent contract to purchase fall out of agreement at higher rates than in previous periods. A corollary to this basic concept involves an increase in price negotiations at the point of contingency removal for those contracts that are conditioned on final approvals.

iii) The ratio of qualified buyers to sellers as measured by the number of offers on existing inventory is waning.

iv) The offers that buyers tender are at prices below previous offers with the relative difference an indicator of the degree of the change. For example if the pre-shift price would yield a cash flow of 6% and the current offers are at prices that yield 8% there is an obvious downward movement in prices.

v) Luxury foreign car dealers experience a rise in early lease terminations from inexperienced investment real estate brokers and over-leveraged developers who try to cut expenses as a result of the reduction in market velocity.

b) In both rapidly appreciating and depreciating markets **only the most active investors and brokers have access to enough data to be able to determine market shifts before the obvious change in selling prices.** As a result of the lack of information it is not unusual for many real estate investors to be ignorant of a market shift or the degree of the shift until the information has migrated to the cocktail circuit.

c) In a perfect world, if there was a buyer barometer that measured the number of buyers, their buying parameters and their degree of motivation, such a device would be the best leading indicator. Buyers are the first to react to market changes and typically trigger market shifts. **Sellers' expectations can lag shifts in buyer motivation by months.** For that reason, it is important for prospective sellers and less active buyers to have contacts within the industry that have access to data concerning recent market trends. Trend information should include what is going under contract not just what is closing. Recent closings may have been under contract for ninety days or longer. In a rapidly evolving market, changes in relative value can be significant in a ninety day period. The best sources for current trend information are high volume investment real estate brokers, title companies that handle commercial transactions and if you are lucky, assorted relatives who are active buyers and sellers of investment real estate. It is doubtful that any of these sources will relate specific deal information prior to any closing but they have the option of discussing trends in prices.

3 How to Determine a Fair or Market Price

a) Pricing of an investment property can be determined by any number of theoretical methods, but the only real test is to have the property effectively marketed.

b) In a market that is appreciating, defining a fair price is generally bracketed by what is on the market and not selling and what has recently sold. In a declining market, what has sold is usually the high range with the low range being somewhere below what has sold. In a down market, it is somewhat irrelevant what is on the market other than identifying that the market is oversaturated with over-shopped, over-priced properties for sale by overly optimistic sellers.

c) Depending on the rate of change in prices, there can be a large gap between a retail price and a wholesale liquidation. In a rapidly appreciating market, it is not uncommon to see unmarketed or poorly marketed properties sell 10 to 15 percent below retail.

d) When market prices decline the volume of transactions contracts rapidly. In markets with low volume, opinions of value based on small samples of previous closings are at best an estimated guess. Such properties need market exposure and a skilled intermediary/advocate representing why the price as presented is justifiable.

e) History has shown that sellers who over-negotiate in a down market usually end up in a series of escrows with each new conditional agreement at a lower price than the previous one. Pessimists are the best negotiators/sellers in a down market. They typically assume the worst will happen, take what is on the table and close the transaction promptly. In a down market, when the need to sell is acute, optimists should not be put in charge of property dispositions.

Selecting the Right Broker 4

a) The ability of a broker to add value is a function of their familiarity with the market, their capability of accessing information, their ability to identify how to reposition a property to create greater value, their ability to find properties for sale and their potential for sourcing buyers. They should also have the ability to effectively persuade the entity they don't represent that their client's position is reasonable and merits action. This last ability is becoming rarer among an expanding community of marginal brokers. It is also a skill that can offer the greatest added value, especially in markets or with deals that lack momentum.

b) The broker's track record is important, but not as critical as how they did their deals. There is a group of brokers with relatively good resumes whose main function in representing their client has been that of a courier of documents. During extended periods of income property appreciation, the velocity in the investment real estate market becomes strong enough that the momentum of motivated buyers and sellers makes it possible for the United Parcel Service broker to flourish. It is important to contact the parties that the broker represented and determine what the broker's role was in the transaction. Responses such as "our broker was very responsive," and "he/she was very effective at delivering documents," are not the responses you want. Certainly the comment that "the broker's role was mostly protecting their fee" is another warning sign.

c) Many experienced income property investors will challenge a broker to defend their track record and question them intensely about how the business was executed. This devil's advocate interaction with a broker can tell you a great deal about how the broker will react when challenged. Brokers who lamely explain their capabilities or limply defend their positions will be weak and flaccid in representing their clients. A broker should be able to effectively explain and assertively defend what value he or she will add.

d) For prospective sellers, if a broker beauty pageant is being used as part of the process of selecting a broker, be aware that the 'big claim quotient' is a malady that is rampant within the industry. Ask for references and talk to other owners who have actually experienced what a broker did (if anything) to benefit the client. Although such research takes time there is usually a good laugh somewhere in the process.

e) Selling clients should beware of brokers promising shotgun marketing. Broker to broker to broker marketing is much like the old parlor game where the first person in line memorizes a short written statement and secretly whispers the statement to the next person in line. The information is passed along in similar verbal fashion until it reaches the last person. It is virtually guaranteed that the statement as it began will be very different when recited by the last person in the queue. With the parlor game experiment in mind, the closer the information is to its source, the better it is for both seller and prospective buyers. Brokers whose marketing programs are centered on contacting other brokers offer marginal utility and a low value-added service since identifying other qualified brokers is not that difficult in this age of information transparency. If, for whatever reason, the decision is made to list with a broker whose core marketing program is contacting other brokers, in such situations the bulk of the fee should be reserved for the broker who represents the buyer.

f) Lists of active local brokers can be obtained from:

   i) **www.loopnet.com** by checking the brokers who have the most listings in the target area.

   ii) **www.costar.com** CoStar is a fee service that requires some familiarization and training but it has extensive data on broker activity by locale, property type and size.

   iii) Local title companies that handle commercial transactions.

   iv) Local commercial real estate appraisers.

   v) Attorneys who specialize in real estate law.

   vi) "Income Property For Sale" section of local newspapers or the Wednesday edition of *The Wall Street Journal.*

Real Estate Partnerships Sponsor vs. Investor: Who Gets What?

5

a)   The business of taking on partners is one of the most common ways that smaller investors can share in the economies of scale of larger properties and also benefit from the experience of the sponsor. It is also a method by which an investor/sponsor can compete for larger deals. The primary questions are who puts up the money, what are the fees to the sponsor and how are the cash flow and the proceeds from a sale distributed? The most common form of group investing today is the limited liability company—LLC. In a typical LLC, the sponsor is the managing partner and the investors are the shareholders. The primary benefit to the investor is the limited liability feature of the LLC. If the LLC is properly constituted and operated, the investor's liability is limited to their initial investment.

b)   Although there are countless variations, **the following are typical financial relationships between the sponsor and investor.**

i) The investor would typically contribute anywhere from 75 to 100 percent of the cash investment with 95 to 99 percent being typical.

The sponsor would invest the difference.

ii) The sponsor would typically get an add-on administrative (brokerage) fee equal to 2 to 4 percent of the price paid at closing.

iii) For properties that require off-site management, a management fee of 3 to 5 percent of the collected gross income would be paid monthly to the sponsor out of the income from the property.

iv) On sale the sponsor would get a disposition fee of 2 to 5 percent of the property's price.

v) Finally, when the property is sold the sponsor would get a percent of the profits. The percent is a function of the sponsor's track record and how high the preferential return is to the investor.

vi) The investor would get a preferential (PREF) return based on a certain annual percentage of their investment.

vii) The PREF is typically paid out of cash flow and distributed quarterly. If the cash flow from the property is insufficient to cover the distribution, most sponsors reserve the right to not pay the PREF. In those situations the PREF would accrue at simple interest rates.

viii) When the property is sold, the investor would receive their original investment plus any accrued PREF not previously distributed. The remaining amount would be split with the sponsor based upon an agreed formula.

For PREFs in the range below 9 percent, the profit would usually be split 50 percent to the sponsor and 50 percent to the investor. For PREFs 10 percent and above the sponsor split of the profits would typically go to the 55 percent to 60 percent range with the sponsor getting the additional profit participation in exchange for the higher investor PREF.

Joint Ventures with Institutional Partners — 6

This annotation is included to show the contrast between institutional investors and private party investors relative to sponsor fees and compensation. This annotation is not referenced anywhere in the investor narratives.

The following are examples of typical financial relationships between large and well established sponsors and large institutional investors. In the examples it is assumed that the institutional investor is contributing all or almost all the equity.

a)   Fees paid to the sponsor typically include an up front fee of up to 1 percent of the purchase price.

b)   For properties that require intensive off-site management, there would be management fees in the range of 2.5 to 3 percent of collected revenue. The sponsor may be able to make a small amount of additional profit off of this fee assuming their costs of internal management are less than fee paid. If property management is outsourced the sponsor may be able to get a small override on the fee paid to the third party manager.

c)   In some situations the sponsor may be able to negotiate an asset management fee. Such a fee is based on a percent of the asset value paid annually to the sponsor. Such fees are usually one-half of one percent of asset value or less. Some institutional investors limit the fee to the amount of equity investment, which may be a much smaller fee if the property is leveraged.

d)   In terms of profit participation, the sponsor would split the profits with the investor based on certain formulas. The typical formula would result in a 50/50 percent split after a 10 percent preferred return to the investor. Waterfalls are also common with investors receiving the bulk of initial returns and the sponsor receiving increased participation (promote) as the asset achieves higher levels of returns. The rate varies depending on the institution's degree of investment motivation and the strength of the sponsor. Another example is a lower preferred return of 8 percent to the investor but a 60/40 percent split of profits with the 60 percent going to the investor. Most investors are not underwriting deals at total returns less than in the teens (levered deals). In the event the deal does not achieve the hurdle rate of return (teens vs. 8 percent stated above), the investor gets to look-back to the sponsor's promote in order to help achieve their yield.

e) Although infrequent, the sponsor may be able to negotiate a 1 percent disposition fee with that fee being a percent of the price paid when the project is sold. Such fees are becoming less typical since there is no alignment of interests between the investor and the sponsor. If the sponsor is taking fees off the top of a sale that are unrelated to the profitability of the project the investor's return is obviously diluted.

7 The Politics of Developing

a)   Prior to entering into the battle of building permits, the developer should have a general knowledge of a city's political attitude towards development. Municipalities with extreme anti-development histories should be avoided.

b)   If the political environment is acceptable and if the development potential of the project is reasonable, the following steps should be a prelude to final approval.

    i) Tie up the land with a conditional offer to purchase. One of the conditions would include getting approval from the city to build the project.

    ii) Interact with those in city government that will have an influence on the acceptability of the project.

      (1) Meet with the highest approval authority within the city to see what they want in terms of project features.

      (2) Meet with all the departments that will have input into the project—planning commission, building department, division of public works, planning department, etc.

iii) Meet with any neighbors to the project to discuss plans and determine if there will be problems.

iv) Have an architect develop concept plans based on the political and neighborhood input.

v) Get preliminary bids from three or four contractors to get an idea of costs.

vi) Take the preliminary plans to the appropriate governmental departments.

vii) After getting preliminary approvals or very firm positive head-nods, have a full set of plans drawn.

viii) Select a contractor and get bids for construction.

ix) Go to the city for final approvals.

x) If you have a religious affiliation, pray to your deity of choice.

8 Miscellaneous Development Risks

a) **Environmental issues are of increasing importance.** The Endangered Species Act has opened the door to a new set of challenges for developers.

b) Land that has never been worked or tilled requires close investigation. Various critters may have de facto title to the land as a result of their right to life, liberty and the pursuit of nesting.

c) Ground squirrels may indicate the presence of a burrowing owl. Borrowing owls are a prime ally of anti-development groups. The need to relocate the borrowing owl to a new and comparable location can be a challenging endeavor —that's assuming that the owls and their legions of environmental allies agree to the relocation.

d) Sites that have been previously developed offer added risk, especially if there is the threat of old wells and buried gas or diesel tanks. The potential presence of such underground threats leads to a developer affliction known as alopecia (hair loss).

Off-Site Management: Third Party Vendors

9

a) There are problems and benefits in hiring third party, off-site managers. **The problems include:**

i) In order to understand the third party management, it is helpful to understand what drives bottom line profitability of the business. Third party managers make significant investments in personnel, accounting systems, legal compliance efforts, etc. In order to compete effectively in the marketplace, these relatively fixed costs are amortized over as many units as possible. As a result, fee-motivated property management companies are driven to add incremental business. In other words, by amortizing their fixed costs over a larger base of units, management company profitability is enhanced. Therefore, property management companies are usually quite good at getting the business. Regional and senior officers within the management company are generally comprised of marketing types more skilled at selling than at the more fundamental daily tasks of property management. As they expand and take on more clients, it may be challenging for an owner to remain at the top of their preferred client list. Generally speaking, the lower you are on the preferred list the lower the level of service and responsiveness. If your account is smaller, your ability to adroitly nag and sell the concept of future business in exchange for today's responsiveness will be very important.

ii) In order to maintain their growth and be able to offer better compensation opportunities for their employees, independent management companies are forced to grow, which means they must compete for business in an environment of shrinking fees. That lowers their ability to provide services since they have to stretch limited staffs over a larger number of managed assets. The result is that their capacity to offer a qualitative service is influenced by a precarious balance between revenue pressure and the prospect of increased expenses.

b) **The benefits include:**

i) If they are large enough, it is highly likely that they have systematized the back office function so that the process of revenue collection and bill payment can be efficiently and cost-effectively executed.

ii) They act as a legal buffer since they are the employer of all off-site personnel. They may also be the employer of the on-site staff depending on who is writing the on-site salary checks. Some landlords pay the on-site staff rather than delegate that function to third-party managers. In that situation the landlord is usually legally responsible for the on-site employees.

iii) Since they are in the business, it is likely that they are aware of the latest problems and opportunities within the industry which should translate to benefits for those who are using their services.

iv) They can be fired and replaced more easily than an in-house team.

v) A truly strong relationship between the management company and owner can result in useful information about additional investment opportunities, under-managed assets, etc.

10 An In-House Property Management & Leasing Organization

a) The advisability of establishing a proprietary off-site management and leasing operation is dependent on a number of important issues.

   i) Your portfolio must be large enough to justify hiring full time employees

   ii) You have to make the commitment of putting an in-house organization in place that will require constant attention. Off-site management is a thankless task that needs senior management focus.

   iii) You should put in place a long term compensation plan for your management team. Typically the compensation plan would include an equity component but only for those companies that have a significant portfolio of properties under management.

   iv) You have to be able to make the assumption that the value you extract from an in-house team will justify your time, expense, and risk of setting up such an entity. Value would be defined as a qualitatively better operation that maximizes your ownership goals.

b) The fact that the majority of larger real estate portfolios are managed by internal operations is a testimony of the benefits of a company-owned management business. A well run and responsive in-house property management/leasing team can justify the costs when comparing their added value above that of a third party manager with shifting priorities and intrinsic business problems. In-house management should also result in greater alignment of investment objectives with on-the-ground property management execution.

c) The operation of a third-party management company is typically a low margin business. To have as a goal to form an internal management company to increase profits through outside management fees is not sound thinking. There is considerable pressure to reduce off-site management fees. What once might have been a more profitable business is now a low margin, very competitive, mature business.

d) Off-site management taken in-house has also become more challenging with the increase in the number of legal issues relating to employment and with the increased costs of health insurance and other employment costs and taxes. One or two wrongful termination suits will ultimately raise costs and challenge all but the most committed owners.

11 Working with Off-Site Managers (Internal or Third-Party)

a)   **An annual budget must be established between the off-site management company and the owner.** The management company should propose a budget that would include detail down to specific line items of income and expenses. The owner should challenge the budget assumptions to see if the management company understands the project and has conducted adequate research. The new budget should be compared to the previous operating results of the property and also compared to industry norms. Additionally, owner and manager should come to agreement regarding required or projected capital expenditures, approval processes, etc.

b)   **Monthly meetings should be scheduled between the owner and the property management company.** The main goal of the meeting is to compare the budget with the results and take corrective measures if the budget is not being met. Additionally the monthly discussion should include a market study to determine competitive rental levels.

c)   **Quarterly the owner or the owner's representative should inspect the property and conduct their own market study** to verify that the rents are competitive and that the property is being maintained and operated consistent with their short and long term goals. It is not unusual for management companies to keep rents low so that the on-site manager can report high occupancy. This approach will not maximize revenue. Many management companies will also be tempted to cut costs to reach budgetary net income goals. The cost cutting may not be consistent with the longer term viability of the project.

d)   The Institute For Real Estate Management (IREM, irem.org) publishes information that serves as a benchmark for comparisons of income and expenses for apartment, retail, and office projects. The Building Owners and Management Association (BOMA, boma.org) is another outstanding source for data on office projects. The International Council of Shopping Centers (ICSC, icsc.org) is the industry sponsored group for research and information concerning retail and shopping center projects. All three organizations require membership and a fee for full access to their data. They also publish information available to the public but without the discounts that members enjoy.

12 Building an Internal Staff

a) Selection of the right candidate for any position is of critical importance. The topic is too lengthy for a bullet-point discussion. Recommended reading would include: *Topgrading: How Leading Companies Win by Hiring, Coaching and Keeping the Best People,* by Bradford D. Smart; *High Impact Hiring: How to Interview and Select Outstanding Employees,* by Del J. Still; *96 Great Interview Questions to Ask Before You Hire,* by Paul Facone; *Interviewing: More Than a Gut Feeling,* by Richard S. Deems; and *The Executive's Manual of Professional Recruiting,* by John Truitt.

b) One of the main issues in building an organization is the option of hiring experienced candidates vs. hiring less experienced people and having the proprietor or a senior manager train the new inexperienced employee. For most mission critical positions that require immediate expertise, hire the experience! A mix of battle scarred veterans and new trainees is typical in most growing real estate organizations.

c) It is important to hire competent new employees who can learn at the arm of an experienced practitioner. The added expense of hiring and training will be rewarded with longer retention of such employees; they will be taught the company way without preconceptions and finally the company will have an evolving cadre of managers that reflects the goals of the founder.

Employee **13**
Compensation
Plans

a)   Appropriate compensation plans should be performance based. Salaries should be at subsistence levels for employees whose activities directly impact the profitability of their project. Bonuses should be expressed as a percent of salary with a potential bonus pool established at the beginning of a planning cycle.

b)   Bonus potential from 25 to over 200 percent of the base salary is typical. The higher the bonus potential the closer the relationship between the specific tasks of the employee and the impact of their decisions on the profitability of their project.

c) Bonus compensation should have two components: one part related to company performance and the other relating to that part of the project the employee can influence. The ratios between the part attributed to company performance and individual performance vary widely, but most bonus programs are heavily weighted toward individual performance.

d) Bonuses must be performance based and rewarded on the basis of measurable, quantifiable goals.

e) For employees whose job function is difficult to attach to specific profit-related activity, their bonuses should be proportionally smaller and impacted by both company profitability and also linked to subjective goals aimed at increasing specific job related skills.

f) Quarterly reviews and progress reporting for all employees are necessary to insure that the bonus program is influencing behavior. An employee who is not making their quarterly goals has to be made aware that their shortfall is negatively impacting their bonus and possibly their future employment.

g) Generally speaking, fractional bonuses paid during the year are not recommended since most real estate projects may not have monthly or quarterly bottom line results. That said, bonuses should be budgeted, reviewed, and paid on an annual basis.

Employees as Equity Partners 14

a) If you are hiring an experienced employee whose track record clearly demonstrates that they can immediately add to the profitability of your organization, it is wise to offer them equity. **By offering equity, you will more closely align their interests to yours,** they will be less susceptible to the temptations of short-term compensation, and more likely to focus on building a long term, profitable business. Any equity should vest over a period of time since it makes little sense to grant equity until there is a measurable contribution. As an example, if someone is offered ownership of the company when they are hired, the amount offered should be earned and granted over a three or four year period. The vesting is generally proportional so that during a four-year vesting period, 25 percent of the total would vest each year.

b) **The new equity partner should be required to invest cash** even if it is at a discounted price per share. In discounted price situations an accountant or tax attorney should advise both parties of potential tax liabilities.

c) **Employees who are "home-grown" should also be considered for equity.** Since equity should be related to long term contributions, an employee would typically have to be with the firm for three or more years and during that time demonstrate that they have significantly added to the profitability of the operation. After the appropriate time and contribution, they should be offered equity that would vest over the next three or four years.

d) **Other criteria for considering whether someone should become an equity partner** include:

   i) **Would you trust them with your wallet?** If there is a question about a fiduciary relationship, don't offer equity.

   ii) **Is the person's interest aligned with your goals?** If for instance an employee wants to have a steady nine-to-five job without stress or responsibility, they are probably not an equity candidate for the typical real estate business. If someone wants to strike it rich quickly and get on to some other endeavor they should not be an equity partner, unless that is also the goal of the organization.

   iii) **All potential equity partners should endorse and be committed to the short and long term goals of the organization.**

   iv) **Will the new partner fit in with the existing shareholders** or will they create unnecessary friction? If there is the perception that the new partner didn't adequately contribute to the growth of the organization and if the new partner's equity participation results in the dilution of his or her peers the risk of bringing in a new partner can be significant.

Buying Investment **15** Real Estate Below Construction Costs

a)   There are buyers who have built considerable real estate fortunes buying property below construction costs. There are some advantages and some drawbacks in employing this strategy.

b)   The primary advantage is that by buying below construction costs, the buyer is able to rent the property for less and still earn a reasonable return on investment. For example, if an investor purchases a 55,000 square foot office building for $150 per square foot, the price would be $8,250,000 (55,000 multiplied by $150). Assuming the investor wants a minimum return of 8 percent on their investment, they could rent the property net of expenses for $660,000 per year ($8,250,000 multiplied by 8 percent). The annual rent per square foot would be $12

($660,000 divided by 55,000). If the cost of new construction is $200 a square foot, and if a developer was to build a 55,000 square foot building, their cost would be $11,000,000. If they wanted a similar 8 percent return they would have to rent their building for $880,000 net of expenses. Their annual rent per square foot would be $16 which is 33 percent higher than the building that was purchased below construction cost.

c) The obvious rental advantage is not the only benefit. By buying below construction costs and being in the market with very competitive rents, the ability of other developers to bring new product to the market has greater risk. Assuming that some developers border on being rational, in the short term the added risk could preempt a few new competing projects from being built. Another advantage is that when an improved rental market does justify new construction, the upside in future rent should be much greater for the below-construction cost investor.

d) The final advantage is that lenders are usually more willing to lend on a building with a lower cost-per-square-foot because of the perceived lower risk. This is presuming that the rent from the project adequately covers the debt service.

e) The problem with the below-construction-cost plan is that if this is the investor's only strategy, many favorable opportunities to purchase can be missed. The availability of below reproduction cost deals is usually only prevalent during weak or down markets. Some of the most lucrative buying opportunities are from purchasing at or above construction costs in supply-constrained markets that are at the start of an up cycle. The below-construction-cost investor tends to miss such opportunities.

Portfolio Management 16

a) Portfolio management involves evaluating the overall risk of a property or group of properties and comparing the risk profile with the anticipated growth in future revenue and value.

b) If an investor is fortunate enough to have their property in a location that has historically avoided abrupt and lengthy down cycles, and where the up cycles are more frequent and with greater amplitudes, then portfolio management is probably not as critical but still necessary.

c) For properties in markets that have greater price fluctuations as a result of larger swings in rents, for those properties in markets that are demographically evolving toward greater risk profiles, for those properties located in areas that are susceptible to overbuilding, and for those properties that are becoming economically obsolete, it is very important to exercise astute portfolio management.

d) The income potential for every property evolves as markets change. The evolution can take months, years, decades, and possibly centuries. Even some of the most favored coastal locations can erode both figuratively and literally as nature, and the nature of investing, change. As an example assume a draconian rent control ordinance is passed. The combination of rent control and confiscatory restrictions on alternative use can change location, location, location to should-have-sold, should-have-sold, should-have-sold. Regardless of current optimism, each property in a portfolio should be analyzed economically, demographically, cosmetically, functionally, politically, and competitively to determine if selling or exchanging the asset for a property with better fundamentals makes sense.

Leverage and Financing Income Property

17

a) The degree of leverage permitted by lenders is influenced by two principal factors—the relationship between loan amount and market value, and the relationship between annual debt payments and the property income.

b) The relationship between loan amount and market value, referred to as Loan to Value (LTV), is reasonably well understood. Lenders will typically lend up to 75 to 80 percent of the market value, established by independent appraisal and the lender's loan committee appraisal guidelines. More restrictive appraisal guidelines can result in maximum LTVs of 60 percent or less. From the perspective of the lending institution, the lower the LTV the less risk as the borrower has more equity in the property. Lenders typically often reduce the interest rate on low LTV loans in recognition of the reduced risk.

c) The relationship between annual debt payment (principal and interest) and net operating income (NOI) is commonly referred to as the debt coverage ratio (DCR). This widely used benchmark measures a property's ability to cover regular mortgage payments and is calculated by dividing the NOI by a property's annual debt payment.

d)   **Debt Coverage Ratio:**

$$\frac{\text{Net Operating Income} \quad \$100,000}{\text{Annual Debt Payment} \quad \$80,000}$$
$$= 1.25$$

i) DCR requirements for lending institutions may range from 1.10X to 1.30X or higher. From the perspective of the lending institution, the higher the DCR, the less risk as there is more income available to cover the debt payments.

ii) Lenders estimate the NOI by using current market rents less market vacancy and typical operating expenses. These numbers are compared with the actual historical results, operating results from similar properties financed by the lender and confirmed by the results of the property appraisal.

iii) Once the NOI is known, the lender divides the figure by the permitted DCR to arrive at the annual debt payment for the proposed loan.

e)   **Annual Debt Payment:**

$$\frac{\text{Net Operating Income} \quad \$100,000}{\text{Debt Coverage Ratio} \quad 1.25}$$
$$= \$80,000$$

ii) The size of the loan that can be supported by the annual debt payments is a function of the loan amortization period and the interest rate for the loan. The lender selects an appropriate amortization period, based on the age and quality of the building and an appropriate interest rate—either the actual interest rate for fixed rate loans or a stabilized interest rate for variable rate loan.

ii) Once the amortization period and interest rate are known, the annual debt constant is determined by referring to a mortgage constant reference chart or one can calculate the monthly payment for a loan of $1,000, convert the result into an annual payment (multiply by 12), divide the result by $1,000, and express as a percent. By illustration, a 6 percent loan amortized over 30 years has annual payments equal to 7.2 percent of the loan amount. The annual debt constant is divided into the annual debt service and the result is the loan amount:

f)   **Loan Amount:**

Annual Debt Payment	$80,000
Annual Debt Constant	7.2%
	= $1,111,111

i)As the example illustrates, a property with a NOI of $100,000 will support a loan of $1,111,111 assuming a 1.25X DCR, a 6 percent interest rate and a 30 year amortization. The property creates 25 percent more income (NOI) than is required to cover the annual debt service.

ii)   If the debt coverage is reduced, the loan amount increases. By illustration, a lender that requires a minimum DCR of 1.10 and uses a 7.2 percent loan debt constant (6 percent amortized over 30 years) will lend $1,262,626.

Net Operating Income	$100,000
Debt Coverage Ratio	1.10

= $90,909/7.2% = $1,262,626

g)   The DCR acts as a buffer between the property income and the mortgage payment. As DCRs approach 1.0X, there is less of a buffer and a correspondingly higher risk that the income from the property will be unable to cover the mortgage payments.

h)   As a result, lenders are generally reluctant to utilize DCR of less than 1.10X on a stabilized basis. Where the borrower has a strategy to increase the DCR by improving the Net Operating Income, lenders will occasionally reduce their DCR requirements to 1.00X (break-even debt coverage), on the understanding that the borrower will improve the NOI within a given time period. On situations where the loan is made for a short period of time, with the expectation that the borrower will secure permanent financing from another source, the loan is called a bridge.

i) In exchange for the increased risk of a 1.00X— 1.10X DCR, lenders typically increase the interest rate and/or loan points. Conversely, on properties with 1.35X or higher DCR, lenders reduce the interest rate on the loan, or provide other incentives, like waiving escrows for property taxes and/or insurance.

j) In markets with a high risk of competition from additional supply or in a market with a volatile employment base (demand) lenders often increase their DCR requirement, or use other strategies to accomplish the goal of a more conservative loan. These strategies may include using an artificially high interest rate or shorter amortization period (both increase the debt constant) or using a higher market vacancy factor or higher operating costs relating to turn-over (both reduce the net operating income).

18 Identifying Apartment Projects That Have Been Hot-Rodded For Sale

a) The best indicator of a project that has been accelerated in its rental growth to attain price maximization can be identified by comparing rental records over the last twelve month period. Rents can be accelerated by providing the tenants with an improved unit which can be done through various upgrades to the apartments. Rental increases from this type of expenditure are usually durable and don't need to be discounted.

b) There are other ways of increasing rental rates that are not favorable for a new owner. Such methods all fall into the broad category of concessions, either of the monetary or non-monetary type. These include lowering the screening requirements of tenants or admitting tenants with pets (generally the larger the pet the more rent that can be charged—beware of St. Bernards roaming the property), permitting early move-ins, side concession agreements, offering incentives such as free consumer goods (TVs, IPods, digital cameras, computers, George Foreman Jumbo Indoor/Outdoor Grills, etc.) in exchange for higher rents.

c) Another method, such as offering free rent disguised through the difference in move-in dates and the effective date of the lease, is deceptive and misleading. In such situations the tenant would move in and not pay rent since the lease is dated one or two months after the move-in date. The lease would have an artificially high contract rent obtained in exchange for the free rent. Such a technique is more difficult to identify.

d) Careful due diligence of the last twelve months operating records, checking rental records, questioning the resident manager about recent changes in rental policy, a detailed examination of miscellaneous expense items and a unit-by-unit comparison of the last twelve months of rents and occupancy levels will usually reveal projects with pumped-up rents.

e) Apartment projects that have had rents artificially inflated have to be discounted back to what the price should be given normal and prudent rental policies.

19 Apartment Rehab Costs and Payback Formulas

a) The option of improving the property with the goal of increasing rents and cash flow are important factors in utilizing active management to substantially improve investment returns.

b) Improvements should not be attempted unless occupancy and rents can be increased as a result of the money expended. An exception would be health and safety expenditures that should always be made to keep the project up to current codes. Another exception would include cosmetic improvements that may not necessarily relate to immediate increases in income but are necessary to keep the physical structure esthetically competitive with other projects in the area. Maximizing curb appeal should be a high priority for attracting and keeping a better quality of tenant.

c) As a general rule every dollar of improvement should be recouped through additional net operating income within a three to four year cycle. Returns on investment that take longer to recoup than three to four years are generally not additions since many improvements have limited useful lives. Some capital expenditures have paybacks in the form of reduced operating expenses. These include separate metering, capital improvements that reduce annual repair, and maintenance costs.

d) The return of costs over the three-to-four year period becomes less important if the goal is to increase income with the thought of quickly re-selling the property and moving your equity and profit into a larger property.

e) As an example, assume $50,000 is spent on improvements and it takes four years to recoup the costs through rental increases. This means that on a straight line basis $12,500 (not including the opportunity cost of what could be done with the $50,000 to generate other income) would be recaptured in increased rent each year. The impact on sale of net income that is $12,500 higher is much greater in terms of increasing value over the $50,000 cost. Assuming that an apartment project can be sold at a 6 percent CAP rate, for every one dollar increase in net income the added value would be over four times that amount ($12,500 divided by 6 percent equals $208,333; $208,333 divided by $50,000 equals 4.2 times). Obviously the entire $12,500 would not fall to the net income, but most buyers will not take the $50,000 and deduct the proportional expense from the annual net income. This creates the value-added impact of appropriate capital improvements.

20 Conversion of Apartments to Condominiums

a)   During periods of increased demand for for-sale housing, the conversion of apartments to condominiums becomes popular.

b)   The ability to convert is impacted by city ordinances and political attitudes towards condo conversion. Certain cities prohibit or severely restrict the ability to convert rentals to condos.

c)   When condo converters buy apartments they will typically pay a price that is at a 25 to 35 percent discount from the aggregated condo sale prices. For instance, if a 50-unit apartment project can be purchased and sold as condos, the converter will calculate the sale of the 50 units as condos and then take a 25 to 35 percent discount from that amount to determine the price they will pay for the project as an apartment.

d)   Most converters will not purchase an apartment to convert unless they are assured that the conversion is technically and politically possible.

e)   Inadequate parking is usually the greatest physical restriction on converting apartments to condominiums.

Professional 21 Apartment Management

a) For a 100+ unit property, a professional, full time, off-site management company would generally need to earn a floor fee of about $25,000 a year to justify taking on a project. In general, $25,000 is adequate to cover the property management company's allocated fixed portion of internal accounting/back office and regional managerial costs.

b) Assuming a management fee of 2.5 percent of the collected revenue, annual collected project revenues of $1,000,000 would generate a $25,000 annual property management fee (consistent with the floor fee above). For smaller projects the fee can get as high as 5 percent. As an example, the same $25,000 a year can be obtained from an apartment complex collecting $500,000 in rent if the management fee is 5 percent.

c) Part-time, off-site management companies could be hired for less than $25,000 a year, but at some risk. In this scenario, an investor is likely to get part-time expertise and part-time attention with part-time managers. For example, it is not unusual to find certain real estate brokers who might also offer off-site property management services to their clients as part of the process of doing business and in hopes of getting future sales. Such a service is usually both off-site and off in terms of what a project needs to maximize short and long term results.

22 Market Pricing Portfolio Options for Apartment Investors

In a market with rapidly increasing prices the relative difference in the price of an "A" building and a "B" or "C" building narrows. In such markets it is often an excellent time to sell (trade up) to higher quality buildings in better areas. This concept is especially true if the rents in the lower quality buildings are only 10 to 15 percent below that of "A" buildings. In a declining market, "C" buildings with aggressive rents usually suffer the most. In a typical market the rental difference between "A" and "C" projects would be in excess of 30 percent.

Apartment Investor Vendor List **23**

The following is a list of vendors that an apartment investor should know and have in their database.

    i) The three to five most active apartment brokers in their area.

    ii) An experienced real estate attorney.

    iii) An accountant familiar with the tax aspects of real estate ownership.

    iv) The three to five most active apartment mortgage brokers

    v) A building contractor who is familiar with multi-family construction. The contractor should also be able to supply subcontractors to address various rehab and maintenance issues.

    vi) The names and contacts of the most active direct lenders—those who will deal with principals directly without having to go through a mortgage broker. There is usually a savings in reduced loan fees by being able to go directly to such a lender.

    vii) A title company with a title officer who is

familiar with more complicated investment·
real estate transactions.

viii) A personal banker at a bank large enough
to provide financial assistance when you least
need it.

24 Analyzing Apartment Markets

a) While all markets offer opportunity for profitable
real estate investing, there are several factors to
consider when evaluating relative apartment
market strength.

b) Specific to apartments, the metrics that should be
measured are:

i) Job Growth in Percent (relative position to
national average)—Bureau of Labor Statistics
(**www.bls.gov**), Economy.com.

ii) Job Growth in Absolute Numbers—Bureau
of Labor Statistics, Economy.com.

iii) Construction Forecast (as percent of total
inventory)—Reis Reports (**www.reis.com**),
Property & Portfolio Research (PPR) (**www.
ppr-research.com**).

iv) Household Formation (relative position

to national average)—Bureau of the Census (**www.census.gov**), Economy.com.

v) Housing Affordability Index (relative to national average)—National Association of Realtors (**www.realtor.org**), Bureau of the Census, Bureau of Economic Analysis (**www. bea.doc.gov**), Economy.com.

vi) Home Ownership Rate (relative position to national average)—Bureau of the Census, **Economy.com**.

vii) Median Household Income (as percent of Median Home Price)—Bureau of the Census, National Association of Realtors, **Economy. com**.

viii) Percent Population in Renter Cohorts (ages 18-34 and 65+)—Bureau of the Census, **Economy.com**.

ix) Net Migration (as % of population growth)—Bureau of the Census, **Economy.com**

x) Forecasted Occupancy Movement (measured in year over year change)—Reis, Property & Portfolio Research (PPR)

xi) Forecasted Rent Growth (measured in YOY % change)—Reis, Property & Portfolio Research (PPR)

xii) Forecasted Absorption (as percent of occupied stock)—Reis, Property & Portfolio Research (PPR)

xiii) Year-End Occupancy Rate—Reis, Property & Portfolio Research (PPR)

25 Identifying Stronger Markets

Stronger markets can be identified by:

a)   Above average job growth.

b)   Barriers to new construction (political opposition or zoning restrictions, lack of buildable land, lack of economic feasibility for new housing construction such as high interest rates).

c)   Low housing affordability (high median home price in relation to income).

d)   Above average occupancies (leads to strong rent growth).

e)   Strong demographic trends (in-migration and age of population).

Techniques for Forecasting Apartment Rental Trends   26

a)   When the current market vacancy is above 5 percent, the ability to raise rents is minimal. Vacancy rates at 7 percent and above usually result in a decrease of rents. When the current vacancy is less than 4 percent, it is highly probable that rents can be raised.

b)   In a market where the after-tax costs of home ownership are 20 percent or less of average apartment rents, there is a strong likelihood that renters will be lost to home ownership creating downward pressure on rents for the apartment units with rents that fall within the 20 percent or less range. In markets where the single family home-affordability ratio is going down (fewer people can afford to buy homes) there will be a bias toward new households becoming renters. If the supply of rental housing is stable or grows slower than the rate of renter household formation, vacancy should decline and rents will have upward pressure.

c)   In a market where the new apartment construction pipeline is accelerating but less than the average rate of household formation, there is usually an upward bias on rents. In assessing household growth it is important to remember that the primary rental age groups are in the 18 -29 year old cohort and the 65+ age group.

d)   In any market where the amount of multifamily for-rent building permits exceed 3 percent of the outstanding multifamily stock, the apartment rental market is generally biased towards rental stagnation or declines. The exception would be when household formation is projected to grow at a rate greater than 3 percent. This is assuming that the same ratio of new households that become renters will remain constant. If the market changes so that the majority of new households migrate to ownership, then the growth in household formation would have to exceed 3 percent to maintain stable apartment rental rates.

Best Methods for Sourcing Apartment Renters 27

a) The number one source for renting units has historically been for-rent signs posted on the project. This is not only the most frequent method of attracting renters but it is also the one of the most cost effective. It is important to consider traffic patterns when purchasing or developing apartments. Projects located on a cul-de-sac with little traffic and no window for drivebys can be a difficult project to keep full. Promotional programs to attract tenants will usually result in the prospective tenant driving by the competition. In soft markets, apartments with poor visibility are the most difficult to keep leased and usually have lower rents than comparable high visibility projects. The ancient real estate mantra of "location, location, location" can be substituted by "traffic, traffic, traffic" in terms of how to source apartment renters.

b) The second best source of attracting tenants is through referrals from existing tenants. From an owner's perspective this source can be passive as a result of tenants passing the word because they would like friends and other renters to be in the project. Obviously there will be very little favorable word-of-mouth if the tenant is not satisfied with the project or local management. Tenant referrals can also be encouraged through referral fees paid to tenants. Tenant referrals, especially the free ones, are a very cost effective way to attract other renters.

c) The third most popular and frequent way of attracting tenants is through Internet postings or postings in rental guides. The Internet sites **www.rentnet.com**, **www.rent.com**, **www.apartments.com**, **www.forrent.com**, and **www.apartmentguide.com** are the five most visited. **www.craigslist.com** is also strong in certain apartment rental markets.

d) Newspaper advertising was historically the third best but has slipped to a distant fourth source for attracting apartment renters. Newspaper advertising is also one of the more expensive methods of attracting tenants.

Guarding Against 28 Resident Manager Fraud

Various techniques have been used by apartment resident managers to illegally augment their income. The following are some of the techniques and potential solutions:

a) The most prevalent scam is for a manager to rent a unit off the books. This usually means they collect rent from a tenant while portraying or posting the unit as vacant. The tenant would sign a rental agreement with a company controlled by the manager. The tenant's rent checks would be made out the manager's company. For those tenants who pay in cash, the money would be pocketed by the manager. The best way to prevent the off-the-books scam is to have the off-site manager make unannounced visits to the property, pick up all the keys for units reported as vacant and then go and inspect the units. Not only will this reveal unauthorized tenants but it will also show whether the unit is ready to rent.

b) Another scam is for the resident manager to retain the cleaning deposits and security deposits and post them as having been returned to the tenant. Irrespective of the fact that most states have laws that mandate how cleaning and security deposits are handled, the resident manager would simply try to convince the tenant that they are not entitled to the return of the deposits. If there is no complaint from the tenant, a check for the amount of the deposit would be drawn against the property and deposited in various bank accounts set up by the resident manager. An analysis of checks that were written for returned security deposits would show that the checks went to someone other than the tenant. If questioned, the manager would claim the check was made out to the entity that the tenant designated. A call to the ex-tenant or an investigation into the origin of the bank account might reveal the scam. To prevent such discovery, the manager may have originated the bank account through a friend or relative with a different name. It should be policy that checks for the return of deposits only be made out to the tenant on the lease.

c) In older complexes with coin or cash vending machines that are owned by the apartment complex, the manager may under-report revenue while accumulating a stash of cash. Off-site managers should handle such collections if it is suspected that the resident manager might have a problem handling cash.

d) In those situations where the manager or the wife/husband management team are also responsible for maintenance, the ability to charge for work not done or charge an exorbitant markup for time and personal services is a risk. Visits by the off-site manager should include a verification of completed work and verification that the hourly personnel costs are reasonable. There is a trend in the management business to avoid wife/husband teams. Employ one or the other. Employing both at the same project can create reporting and accountability problems.

e) Managers may enter into verbal agreements with various third-party vendors, such as plumbers, painters, carpet providers, etc., that in exchange for cash kickbacks or other considerations, the manager will give the vendor the opportunity of providing their service. This is a tough one to detect but can usually be discouraged by insisting that any vendors to the project sign an agreement with the off-site management company that all services are provided without incentive payments to local representatives. This must be followed up by calls to the vendors asking the question and reminding them of the signed agreement.

29 Apartment Resident Managers Can They Sell?

a) In a soft market the resident manager's ability to rent units is extremely important.

b) **The owner should test the ability of the manager to sell the apartment to a prospective renter.** The use of professional shoppers (both phone shoppers and on-site shoppers) is one method to differentiate between the order-taker manager and the selling manager. When they are being hired, the resident manager should be made aware that such a technique may be used. If they resent shoppers, they can decline the job. Secretly deploying shoppers when the manager is unaware that such a technique may be used is not the best way to maintain a good relationship with a resident manager. It is also difficult to try to improve their presentation skills unless you can reveal the source of the information.

c) Another technique of testing the manager's selling skills is through a series of role plays. **Video role playing is probably the best simulation method of testing** and providing immediate feedback concerning the manager's verbal skills and selling presence. The role play method is good, especially for training but not as good as a professional shopper at revealing shortcomings in selling skills.

d) **The resident manager should be aware of what the competition offers** and what competition is selling as the advantages of their project. Renters will usually shop a market. If the manager doesn't know what the competition offers it will be very difficult to sell their comparative advantages.

e) **Selling involves some of the following techniques:**

    i) Answering tenant objections. The manager should rehearse and have committed to memory how to effectively handle tenant objections. Asking the manager to fill out a report about the reasons tenants give as to why they don't rent or what their concerns are about the project is the first step. These issues should be reviewed to determine if the objections are real. If there are genuine problems, remedies should be put in place. Most resident managers will say that the tenant feels the rent is too high. Careful rent surveys of the competitors will answer the question. If rents are competitive it is an indication that the managers sales skills may be lacking.

    ii) As part of the process of renting units the manager should make the tenant aware of what may not be obvious in terms of tenant benefits. For instance, not all tenants may recognize the benefits of the location of the complex. In addition, the manager should strongly emphasize the benefits that are more noticeable. The manager should never assume the tenant will see or value any benefits.

iii) The manager should make some effort during the interaction with the tenant to close the sale. Without appearing overanxious, the manager should ask if the prospective tenant would like the unit held for them or ask if the tenant would like to fill out a rental agreement. There is an old adage in sales: "Business goes to those who ask and stays where it is earned."

iv) This topic can consume chapters on selling techniques and how to rent apartment units. The Institute for Real Estate Management (IREM) has some excellent publications on the topic with one of the best being *Practical Apartment Management—Fifth Edition.*

Determining Apartment Rental Rates   30

a)   The asking rent and ultimately the collected rent are critical dynamics in owning and operating apartments

b)   Rents should not be set by the resident manager. Rents should be set through a discussion between the resident manager and the owner or third party manager. Resident managers who receive dictated rents without providing input usually have a built-in bias against what is their most important task—justifying the rent to the tenants. Rents set solely by the resident manager tend to be at the lower end of the rental spectrum.

c)   The foundation for setting rents is a market survey that takes into account all the features and benefits that will have value to a tenant. It is difficult establishing which specific features and benefits relate to what tenants will pay but generally speaking premiums can be charged for the most significant items that are associated with tenant security or convenience. A survey of tenants by a large institutional owner revealed that there were two features for which they would pay a reasonable premium. Those features were in-the-unit washer/dryer combinations and garages. Depending on the location and the tenant profile, broadband access is becoming a more important amenity. Swimming pools and recreation rooms were rated among the lowest in terms of features that would induce tenants to pay higher rents.

d) Setting standard rents for categories of units such as having all 2-bedroom, 2-bath units at the same rent is not advisable. Premiums should be charged for units with views, units closer to parking, units with higher ceilings, units with special features such as upgraded carpeting, etc. Projects with standardized rental levels for similar units are usually not being operated at optimum income levels.

e) A monthly review of rental activity is important. The upper end of the market should be tested by experimenting with higher asking rents. If there is no or minimal vacancy, the complex is probably not maximizing its revenue potential. For those units that don't rent, where there has been adequate traffic of qualified renters, the off-site and resident manager teams should look at the various options. Typically a rent reduction or rental concession such as free rent will solve the problem—assuming that the resident manager is effective at selling tenants to rent units.

Financing the Typical Suburban Office Development Project

31

a) The developer will typically have to pay cash for and take title to the land prior to obtaining a construction loan.

b) The costs of land are traditionally 20-30 percent of the total project.

c) A construction lender will typically provide financing for the balance of the costs of construction.

d) Construction loans are almost always recourse loans with personal liability.

e) It should be the goal of the developer to pay off the construction loan as soon as permanent financing is available. It may be possible to get pre-commitments on permanent financing based on the project achieving certain income goals.

32 Leasing Ideas and Promotions for Leased Investments

a) Free rent can be offered to induce a tenant to rent space. The free rent should be at the end of each twelve month period. For example free rent in the 12th, 24th, and 36th month could be offered to convince a reluctant tenant to sign a lease.

b) Additional tenant improvement allowances given over the standard are used as concessions to get a tenant to sign a lease—it is advisable to keep higher tenant improvement allowances (TIs) as a last resort since most TIs are not necessarily reusable if a tenant vacates. It is usually cheaper and more advisable to give free rent as opposed to tenant improvement allowances that are an immediate drain on cash. With the possible exception of financially strong entities, the tenant should contribute towards tenant improvements. This is particularly true if the TIs would have minimal utility to subsequent renters.

c) Pay leasing commissions in excess of the usual rate. Payment of a full commission to tenant rep brokers is typical in a soft market. In this case a commission and a half would be paid with the half going to the broker representing the landlord.

d) Additional incentives can be paid to a broker representing the tenant. Such incentives may include all expense paid trips, cars, various computer equipment, or other consumer goods that would appeal to brokers such as pepper spray or vitamins.

e) In painfully soft markets it is not unusual to pay brokers for having their tenants tour the property. This type of incentive is a desperate measure since such tours can be easily abused by brokers representing weak or questionable tenants. Such a technique will almost always increase tours of the property. It is a sure way to increase costs and a dubious way to increase the rate at which leases are signed.

f) Broker open houses that offer something free to tenant rep brokers who attend is an old standard to get the leasing community to view the space. Typically food and drinks are enough but as other panic stricken, vacancy plagued landlords roll out the hors d'oeuvres it may be necessary to offer entertainment and door prizes.

33 Best Locations for Suburban Office Development

a) Barriers to new construction are very important. It is assumed that you and your development can overcome the following limitations. Such barriers may include:

   i) Political opposition to development;

   ii) Potential environmental issues as evidenced by inordinately high local sales of Birkenstock footwear;

   iii) Lack of developable land;

   iv) Exceptionally high development fees;

   v) A history of local neighborhood opposition to anything relating to development.

b) High automobile traffic combined with good visibility for the project make it easier to lease a project.

c) A neighborhood that is composed of buildings similar in quality and function is desirable. Locating an office building in a poor area is not advisable since it will be much more difficult attracting tenants. Office buildings located between apartment buildings is not desirable since there is a tendency for the apartment tenants to use the office building's parking. Close proximity to junk yards is not good unless you are hoping to fill the building with junk collectors or tenants who have an interest in scrap metal.

d) Proximity to amenities such as restaurants, banks and cleaners is important. Walking distance to such establishments would qualify as a good location.

Multi-tenant Office 34 Buildings and the First Time Office Investor

a) It is with caution that new investors should embark on investing in office buildings that cater to smaller tenants. The biggest problem revolves around the high costs of attracting and installing tenants into their space. Leasing commissions and tenant improvements are very difficult to amortize over short term, three to five year leases.

b) In situations with high turnover costs and a low probability of being able to recoup those costs during an initial lease term, the prospect of having a viable investment are diminished. The additional problem of new tenants probably not being able to utilize the previous tenant's improvements creates constant pressure on maintaining financially viable occupancies. There is also the dreaded possibility of experiencing the very high costs of having to change office floor plans for new tenants. Modifying heating and air conditioning zones to accommodate a new tenant is very expensive.

c)   Office buildings with long-term leases that are occupied by financially strong tenants do not fall into the treadmill syndrome of running in place trying to recoup turnover costs. Be prepared to pay a premium price for such financial luxury.

35 Retail Property Leasing Recommendations

a)   Unless your property is large enough, you should consider hiring an experienced, third-party retail leasing agent. Prospective leasing agents can be identified by driving the area around your project and identifying those who have the most leasing signs. Scouring "For Lease" postings in the local newspaper or on Internet sites such as Loopnet.com can also give you an idea which brokers are the most active. Good retail leasing brokers are in the market every-day and are constantly interacting with tenants who respond to their signs, advertising and Internet postings. There is no practical way a new investor can source tenants as readily and efficiently as an active retail leasing agent. Two to three of the most active, local, agents should be interviewed. The goal of the interview is to become comfortable with the broker and have them present how they are going to source tenants for your project. It is typical that in most localities that there are few leasing brokers who could be described as knowledgeable, competent and caring. That is why it is of critical importance to choose your agent carefully. Also remember when dealing with brokers they get paid when the deal is made. There are those that can look beyond such a conflict of interest and honestly try to maximize the landlord's advantage. Asking for such preferred representation is unreasonable without giving the broker the exclusive right to represent you in leasing the space.

b)   Before hiring the broker ask for and call three or more references.

c)   Hiring a leasing agent is an absolute must if the investor is not within close proximity to their project.

d)   Taking leasing in-house is recommended only for those investors whose portfolios are large enough to justify amortizing the cost of full time employees.

36 Retail Property Management

Similar to the recommendation of hiring a leasing broker, a newer investor should consider hiring an experienced property manager. The property manager will be responsible for tenant relations, maintenance, common area billings and other items such as tax payments, utility payments, etc. Investors who are new to retail investing should meet regularly with the management company to accelerate the process of learning how to effectively execute this part of the business.

Ideas for Leasing the Last 15-20% of a Project

37

The leasing of the last 15 to 20 percent of most retail projects is usually the most challenging. Ideas to accelerate the last-to-lease space include:

a) Pay leasing agents bonus payments for smaller space. A leasing commission of $3.50 a square foot may be appropriate for larger space. Paying up to $7 to $8 or more a square foot may be necessary to lease the last space.

b) Structure the leasing commissions so there is a bonus payment if the leasing is completed in a certain time period.

c) Structure the leasing commission so that there are bonus payments based on attaining certain percentages of occupancy.

d) If project leasing stalls at the end, it may be necessary to change the leasing agent. It is not uncommon for an experienced and senior leasing agent to lose some of their motivation after the larger spaces have been leased, especially if the agent has other more lucrative leasing opportunities in other projects. In those situations it is often better to hire a newer, less-experienced but aggressive agent to lease up the last space.

38 Owning & Operating Convenience Retail Projects

Many retail projects cater to necessity or convenience shoppers. The following are guidelines when dealing with such projects:

a) Location is very important since necessity and convenience centers should be in the traffic path of residential developments

b) Travel patterns to and from work will influence the success of such centers.

c) The number of cars going by a center is an important metric in evaluating the viability of necessity and convenience projects. Automotive traffic counts can usually be obtained from a department within city government. Traffic counts above 25,000 per day are recommended as minimums. Many larger and national tenants catering to necessity or convenience shoppers require higher traffic counts in the 40,000+ car per day range.

d) Accessibility is very important. The going-home side of the street is usually preferred to the going-to-work side. Most grocery and staple shopping is done going home from work. The added advantage of being able to make a right turn into the project, as opposed to a left turn which requires going across traffic, increases the likelihood of attracting shoppers. In addition, when leaving such a project the shopper only has to make another right turn. If a center is on the going-to-work side of the commute, it does not mean it won't be successful. Irrespective of whether a project is on the going-home or going-to-work side, it is important that shoppers who are going in the opposite direction be able to circle back to the project without having to drive an inordinate distance.

Screening Non-credit Retail Tenants

39

a)   Have the operator/proprietor of the business fill out a credit report that mirrors a bank credit report. Your banker should be able to supply a generic credit report.

b)   After receiving permission, contact the operator's bank and inquire about their solvency and credit worthiness

c)   Have the operator put together a resume that contains their history in the retail business.

When analyzing whether to take a risk with a tenant who lacks a history of retailing success, remember that a lack of experience can be partially offset with a large bank account and hefty security deposits.

d)   Ask the proprietor to see his or her business plan. The plan should outline the assumptions of their costs and projected revenue. The plan should address all costs including both start-up and operating costs. Many new-to-the-business entrepreneurs fail to account for adequate start-up costs such as the cost of build-out of the space and carrying costs of the business until revenue becomes sufficient to stop their erosion of cash.

e)   Conduct a personal interview with the proprietor with the goal of determining their degree of experience and the validity of their resume and business plan. Beware of allowing a prospective tenant's unbridled enthusiasm to overcome your required skepticism. The chances of a new and unproven tenant being successful in retailing are one in twenty at best. The chances of a landlord having a viable economic lease depend on how long the tenant can pay rent compared to the landlord's cost of occupancy. A hidden cost of a weak tenant is the loss of synergism with other tenants in terms of generating traffic to the project.

f)   Insist on personal guarantees for leases with tenants who lack a history of success. A competent real estate attorney should be employed to draft the appropriate personal guarantee language since the laws governing personal guarantees vary among states.

g) Once a tenant is in their space, keep in regular contact to see how they are doing. Make it a supportive call, not an interrogation. The first indication of good tenant relations is if they take your call or return it in a timely manner.

Important Retail 40
Lease Provisions

a) Included in the tenant's lease should be a provision that requires them to report gross sales. The tenant's gross sales should be reported not less than quarterly. This report should be part of the lease even if the tenant does not pay additional rent based on a percentage of sales. The goal of this report is to track the tenant's rent as a percentage of sales. The following guidelines compare typical ratios of rents to sales for various retailers. Generally speaking, businesses with higher margins can pay a higher percentage of rent to gross sales. When a tenant's rent-to-gross sales ratio exceeds certain norms, there is a higher risk that the tenant will fail. If you see early signs of trouble, you can take remedial action before the tenant goes lights-out.

i) Grocery stores—rent would be in the 2% to 3% range of gross sales

ii) Large chain stores—5% to 8% of sales

iii) General retail stores—8% to 15% of sales

iv) High markup stores such as jewelry and liquor stores—up to 20% of sales

v) Restaurant—8% to 12% of sales

b)   It is advisable to require the tenant to notify the landlord of their intention to vacate or release the space as early as possible. If, for instance, the tenant must give twelve months notice to vacate, then the landlord's probability of losing rent is minimized. Twelve months notice is not typical in a retail lease unless the lease was originally a long term lease. With five to seven year leases, the requirement to give three to six months notice is more typical. The time period during which the tenant must give notice is an important part of the lease negotiation.

Sign Location and Visibility for Retail Projects

41

a) Signage is very important for retail developments, especially for centers that cater to the necessity and convenience shoppers. This is especially true for centers that lack a major anchor tenant, such as a branded supermarket or drug store.

b) The time it takes for a driver to see and register the name of the tenant should be under five seconds. If a car is traveling at 25 m.p.h., this usually means the sign would have to display the tenant's name in letters that are a minimum of 18 inches in height. Sign regulations in many cities prohibit or limit larger signs so it is important to do the research with the local municipality concerning sign ordinances.

c) Signs become less important for superior locations such as a high traffic, corner location with a signal light. For weaker locations signage increases in importance.

42 Parking Ratios

Parking ratios are important depending on the type of tenant that occupies a center. Typically parking guidelines are referred to as a ratio of parking to improvements. For example, a 20,000 square foot retail building would typically need four to five spaces for every 1,000 square feet of improvements. This means that such a project would need 80 to 100 parking spaces. Restaurant tenants require a higher parking ratio. Their parking requirements would be 10 to 12 spaces for every 1000 square feet of space they occupy. A high ratio of restaurants in a project can create parking problems especially when the restaurant hours of operation coincide with other retail tenants. It is not unusual for many non-restaurant tenants to complain about the lack of parking during peak restaurant hours. When leasing space to restaurant tenants it is important to analyze their impact on parking. For tenants that are more service oriented, such as doctor offices or travel agencies, the requirement might go down to two or three spaces for every 1000 square feet of space.

Retail **43**

Vacancy Issues

a) Vacancies in a retail project are very dangerous, especially if there is a prolonged occupancy problem. Existing tenants don't want vacancies near their store because it is usually an indication of a struggling location or project. Not only do the existing merchants feel at risk in such a situation but the feel of vacant units is detrimental to shoppers who need a consumer's enthusiasm to purchase those point-of-sale, last minute, truly unnecessary retail trinkets.

b) In prolonged vacancy situations it may make sense to rent to the higher risk tenants. This would only be true if all other leasing alternatives have been exhausted and assuming that the costs of finishing the space for the new tenant are minimal.

44 Retail Non- and Late Payment of Rent

a) Non-payment or late payments of rent are issues that need immediate attention. Meet with the tenant and discuss why the tenant is delinquent. Compromise only if it makes sense. Compromises such as short-term reductions in rent or extensions of rental due dates are possible alternatives. Helping the tenant with limited marketing programs such as investing some advertising dollars in exchange for the tenant bringing their rent current is one of many options. If after meeting with the tenant you conclude that the tenant will not survive, take immediate measures to remove them from the project.

b) The only exception might be in those situations where your ability to re-lease the space is highly questionable. In those situations it might make sense to renegotiate a month-to-month lease so that you have the option of being able to re-lease the space if you can find a better tenant. In the interim, rent abatement, forgiveness, or reduction in rent may help the failing tenant maintain their storefront. The problem with this alternative is that putting a 'for lease' sign in the window of the retailer in not consistent with helping the tenant survive. In such situations leasing efforts would be through an in-house leasing team or through an outside leasing broker.

Retail Property Management **45**

a)   Management of a retail project is a very important facet of ownership. Federal Realty is a mammoth shopping center owner that is renowned for their management focus and expertise. Their centers are clean, attractively landscaped, their parking lots are kept in excellent shape, the exteriors of their projects are attractive and well maintained, their management personnel are very responsive to tenant needs, and as a result they have some of the highest occupancy rates and some of the highest rents in the business.

b)   Shoppers want a pleasant experience both emotionally and physically. If prospective shoppers see a run-down, tired, dirty center, they are psychologically less likely to visit the project let alone hang out and spend, spend, spend.

46 Retail vs. Non-Retail Tenants

a) The debate about putting non-retail tenants into a retail shopping center has been going on for years. Putting the Immigration and Naturalization Service in a retail center is probably not the best idea but is one that has been tried by owners of questionable mental acuity. A more difficult choice for many shopping center owners is putting service related tenants in retail centers. Options such as a dentist's office, a travel agency, or a real estate brokerage office are examples of tenants who should probably be in office buildings but may not be able to afford office building rents.

b) If it is deemed appropriate to rent to such tenants (i.e., traditional retail tenants are not forming a line to rent the space) it is best to keep such non-retailers at one end of the project.

Retail Property 47 Branding and Promotions

a)   Branding the center and helping with promotional activities can enhance tenant relations and help retail sales. Holiday decorations put in place from Thanksgiving to the beginning of January help the tenants reap the benefits of the genetic holiday shopping hysteria. Promotional ads for the center during other shopping holidays such as Mother's Day can help tenant traffic.

b)   Spending on promotions and marketing should be accompanied by dialog with each of the tenants to maximize tenant goodwill but also as a methodology of getting feedback from the tenants to see if the promotions have actually helped sales. Most tenants will answer positively since the landlord is spending the money. In such situations the actual results are not that important as long as the tenants feel supported and the costs can be somehow justified.

48 The Cost of Tenant Improvements for a Retail Project

a) The cost of improving a tenant's space has a wide range of options. Generally the higher the cost the better it is to have the tenant pay the amount over what would be a standard build-out. A standard build-out would include taped and ready-to-paint interior walls, electrical outlets in, the ceiling dropped, lighting in place, the concrete floor sealed and ready for floor covering, and finally the heating, ventilating, and air conditioning in and zoned to the appropriate locations within the space.

b) The tenant is typically responsible for furnishings, fixtures and equipment (FFE) and interior décor. It is typical, depending on local customs, to include a tenant improvement (TI) allowance in the range of zero for non-credit tenants to $5 to $10 per square foot of rentable space to well capitalized retail tenants. Some larger chain tenants such as Starbucks would ask the landlord to give them a $10 to $25 per square foot allowance. In such situations the rent would be higher to account for the added costs. Some restaurants and high-end specialty retailers spend (or try to get the landlord to spend) over $100 per square foot for improvements.

Construction and 49 Development Loans for Retail Projects

a)   Construction loans and development loans on shopping centers are almost always subject to personal liability. Loans having personal liability mean that the lender can go after the borrowers personal assets in the event of a default. The ability of a lender to attack a borrower personally is a function of the laws of the appropriate state. It is best to consult a local real estate attorney when dealing with loans involving personal liability.

b)   Loans on development projects will range from 60 to 65 percent of total costs including the cost of the land for developments that lack a credit tenant. With a credit tenant paying a majority of the rent the lender will typically loan from 75 to 80 percent of the total costs of the project. Loan rates will float over LIBOR based on the credit of the income.

50 An Attorney Should be Part of Your Team

a) Attorneys can be an important component of a retail development project. A knowledgeable real estate attorney should be consulted when drawing up leases and reviewing any documents that might impact you or your project. Today the retail business is much more adversarial. It is becoming more common, especially in states with a high per-capita ratio of plaintiff attorneys, to have greater legal risk across an entire spectrum of issues.

b) As an example, one legal tactic is to have failing, deadbeat tenants sue the landlord for misrepresentation. The term misrepresentation can include almost anything that the tenant can claim that the landlord promised. The goal is coerce the landlord with the risk of legal fees and adverse settlements in exchange for discharging the tenant from their obligations under the lease. Proper wording of leases and appropriate tenant communications can reduce the risk of an adverse or perverse legal decision.

Determining Asking Rents 51

a)   Determining the appropriate asking rents for new or vacant space is an art with scientific overtones. The ultimate rent will typically be somewhere between asking rents for comparable projects and rents that have been obtained in competing buildings. This range can be very wide depending on the location of the project, the site layout, the amount of the space being leased, the cost of the build-out, the credit of the tenant, the length of the lease, percentage rent or other cost of living provisions in the lease, and the desperation of either the tenant or the landlord.

b)   Arriving at a formula should be the job shared by the landlord and a competent local retail leasing agent. An in-house leasing agent should have a complete market survey and knowledge of all the competing projects. A spreadsheet of recently executed leases compared to asking rental rates in competing projects will reveal the general range. The trade-off for all the other variables is where the art of a deal is critical. A competent leasing agent can help immeasurably. An incompetent and or uninformed leasing agent can multiply the disaster factor.

52 Continuing Education for Retail Real Estate Investors

It is important for newer retail investors to accelerate their learning process. One of the best sources of information for the retail investor is the International Council of Shopping Centers (ICSC). The ICSC is the largest and probably the best real estate trade group in terms of the value it offers to its members.

Becoming active in the local chapter and participating in local, regional and the national events can rapidly increase the learning curve for new to even the experienced retail investor. The ICSC can be contacted via their web site **www.icsc. org.**

Job Loss in Los Angeles County 53

a) Los Angeles lost 107,000 jobs from 2001 to 2003. Jobs were mainly lost in four employment sectors: Manufacturing, Information, Professional and Business Services, and Trade, Transportation and Warehousing.

b) Orange County lost 500 jobs in 2001.

Job Loss Stats in the Denver Area Mid 1980s to Early 1990s 54

a) Job losses occurred in the Denver MSA in 1985 and 1986, when approximately 5,000 and 19,400 jobs were cut, respectively. This equated to a 0.6 percent decrease in 1985 and a 2.3 percent loss in 1986.

b) Employers again slashed jobs beginning in 2001, when almost 34,400 jobs were cut, a decrease of

2.8 percent. Further reductions ensued in 2002 when 18,000 jobs were cut, a 1.5 percent decline. In 2003, employers reduced payrolls by an additional 27,000 positions, a 2.3 percent drop.

55 Down-Cycle in Houston

a)   Apartments:

i) Vacancy increased from single digits in 1980 to 18.4 percent by 1985.

ii) Vacancy did not post significant improvement until 1989, and steadily declined through 2001, leveling off at 4.6 percent.

iii) The vacancy rate increased and in 2004 surpassed the 10 percent mark, but improvement is expected in 2005.

iv) After falling 15 percent in the early 1980s, asking rents have gradually increased. However, the gap between effective rents and asking rates has expanded over the past few years as concessions became more prevalent.

b)   Retail:

i) Vacancy climbed from single digits in 1980 to

over 20 percent in 1987.

ii) Vacancy then improved through 1999, when it reached 9.4 percent, only to jump 400 basis points over the next two years. It has since receded.

iii) After falling 22 percent in the early 1980s, asking rents have gradually improved, with only minor quarterly reductions realized during the most recent downturn. The average asking rent is now almost double the average reported at the low point in 1987.

c)   Office:

i) Market-wide, vacancy climbed 2,300 basis points between 1980 and 1987, when it reached almost 30 percent, though vacancy in many areas surpassed that level.

ii) Moderate improvement ensued beginning in 1996, with rates reaching 11.1 percent in 2000. Vacancy spiked to over 18 percent in 2003, but has declined slightly since.

iii) Asking rents plummeted by more than 40 percent in the early 1980s, before gaining momentum in the late 1990s, finally surpassing pre-1984 levels in 2001.

56 Negotiating Investment Real Estate Transactions

This topic is a book in itself but the following are some brief recommendations.

a) The degree and scope of the negotiating process should be approached from the perspective of your long-term goals against the backdrop of current market conditions. Although this comment will not benefit the sales of negotiating books, if you find a property that has a reasonable asking price that meets your buying criteria, don't negotiate if the market is appreciating rapidly and if it is probable that there will be other buyers at the table within a short period of time.

b) In normal markets negotiating all reasonable issues is typical and almost expected. The best negotiators use a series of last and final, strategic misrepresentations to see what the other party is willing to concede. Typically two, possibly three, last and finals will allow both parties to feel good about the result.

c) In the process of getting under contract, negotiations should be centered on major issues such as price, terms, good faith deposits, and as a last resort, real estate brokerage commissions.

Generally the better negotiators exchange minor issues for more substantive concessions. In a negotiation it is typical to have a list of must-haves along with a list of would-likes. All of the issues are usually presented to the other party as must-haves. The differences will be sorted out in the give and take.

d) Negotiations that take place after entering into a conditional contract should have some basis in fact that was not revealed prior to going under contract. Asking for concessions of any substantive issues should be associated with new information that impacts the current terms of the deal or the future cash flow of the project. The degree of negotiation should bear a reasonable relationship to the new information. If cash flow is 5 percent less than what was represented, it is not reasonable to ask for a 15 percent price reduction. Such a request falls into the over-negotiator category.

e) If you are an active buyer dependent on access to inventory, establishing a reputation as an over-negotiator is inadvisable. You may benefit in the short-term but long-term you will find fewer sellers and brokers willing to subject themselves to the negotiating tactic du jour.

f) In most markets the investment brokerage community is the primary conduit to properties on the market. If a particular buyer has the reputation of engaging in continual negotiations that often result in non-transaction, they will not be at the top of a brokers go to list. As market transparency increases with more efficient information services, the over-negotiator will find it more difficult to access the best inventory.

g) The use of mediators and/or agents in a negotiation has pros and cons. There is a significant body of evidence that skillful and knowledgeable mediators can facilitate negotiations beyond that of principals negotiating directly. For example, in most businesses involving large compensation packages—such as the top entertainers, professional athletes, and heads of corporations—the negotiations are conducted through mediators or agents. Most legal deadlocks result in a mediator or arbitrator being brought in to resolve the conflict. Some of the best empirical studies and comments on the subject are contained in Howard Raiffa's book, *The Art and Science of Negotiation*, now in its fifteenth printing. The book can be very technical but is one of the few negotiating books that base its recommendations on extensive studies rather than a limited number of personal experiences.

h) As a final note, third-party mediators lacking skills can severely muck up a negotiation. Even though the principals who are negotiating face-to-face may dislike the respective hair styles of their counterpart, they can be better served by negotiating directly rather than being represented by poorly-prepared, inexperienced mediators.

Capitalization Rates **57**

a)   A capitalization rate (CAP) is a ratio used to estimate the value of income producing properties. It is derived by taking the net operating income of a property divided by the sales price or value expressed as a percentage.

b)   A CAP rate is a measure of relative return. If a property has a net income of $100,000 and the price is $1,000,000, the CAP would be 10 percent ($100,000 divided by $1,000,000). The $100,000 of net income yields a 10 percent return on the $1,000,000 price. The lower the CAP the higher the price. Assume a shopping center anchored by a historically profitable, national drug chain is on the market at a 6 percent CAP rate. Assume the project has a net income of $450,000. If this project sold at a 6 percent CAP rate the price would be $7,500,000 ($450,000 ÷ 6 %). If the project were to sell for a 9 percent CAP (assume there is new information that the drug store's CEO fled the country with his administrative assistant prior to the firm filing a surprise bankruptcy) the new price would be $5,000,000 ($450,000 of net income ÷ 9 %).

58 Internal Rate of Return

a) The IRR is typically defined as the rate of return that equates the present value of anticipated future benefits with the present value of the investment outlays.

b) The IRR integrates the concepts of compounding and present value. It represents a way of measuring a return on investment over the entire investment period, expressed as a compound rate of interest.

59 Basis Points Defined

a) A basis point is a unit for measuring rates of return that is equal to 1/100th of 1 percent of yield. Basis points are also known as "bips" and abbreviated as "bps." The relationship between percentage changes and basis points can be summarized as follows: 1 percent change = 100 basis points and 0.01 percent = 1 basis point. So, a loan whose yield increases from 5.0 to 5.5 percent is said to increase by 50 basis points.

b)   As another example, if a 6 percent real estate commission is being negotiated at the closing table and the seller arbitrarily wants to reduce the 6 percent fee by 300 basis points, the new fee would be a either an unfair 3 percent for the perspective of the broker, or a windfall of 3 percent when viewed from the vantage point of the sellers bank account.

Tax Deferred Exchanges 60

a)   Tax deferred exchanges are used by many investors to increase the rate at which they build their real estate portfolios. This is possible as a result of being able to postpone taxes on sale.

b)   Under section 1031 of the Internal Revenue Code, a real property owner can sell their property, defer capital gains taxes and then reinvest the proceeds in a like-kind property. To qualify as a like-kind exchange, property exchanges must be done in accordance with the rules set forth in the tax code and in the Treasury regulations.

c)   The definition of 'like kind' properties is relatively broad. In a 1031 exchange you can exchange any real property for any other real property within the United States or its possessions if said properties are held for productive use in trade or business or for investment purposes.

d)   Examples of like-kind property include apartments, commercial, duplexes, raw land and rental homes. As used in the Internal Revenue Code section 1031(a), the words "like-kind" mean similar in nature or character, notwithstanding differences in grade or quality. It is not necessary to exchange apartments for apartments. Apartments can be exchanged for any of the properties included above, and vice versa. It should be noted that primary residences don't qualify for a like-kind exchange since they are not held for use in trade, business, or investment purposes.

e)   To qualify as a 1031 exchange transaction there are four basic tests. First, the real property you sell and the real property you buy must both be held for productive use in a trade or business or for investment purposes and must be like-kind. Second, the proceeds from the sale must go through the hands of a qualified intermediary and not through your hands or the hands of one of your agents. Third, all the cash proceeds from the original sale must be reinvested in the replacement property—any cash proceeds that you retain will be taxable. And fourth the replacement property must be subject to an equal level or greater level of debt than the relinquished property.

f) There are other criteria that must be met to qualify for a tax deferred exchange. One of the criteria involves the periods during which the exchange has to be completed. The first restriction is the identification period. Within 45 days of selling the exchange property you must identify suitable replacement property or properties. You may identify any three properties as possible replacements for your relinquished property. There are two other rules for nominating replacement properties but the three-or-less rule is used almost exclusively.

g) The second time deadline is the exchange period. During the exchange period the replacement property must be received by the taxpayer. The exchange period ends within the earlier of 180 days after the date on which the taxpayer transfers the property relinquished, or the due date for the taxpayer's tax return for the taxable year in which the transfer of the relinquished property occurs.

h) It is recommended that an attorney specializing in 1031 exchanges be consulted prior to starting the exchange process.

61 Flipping a Property

a) Flipping a property is not a common practice but there are buyers who try to augment their bank account by employing the flip strategy. This strategy is executed to the detriment of the seller.

b) **Flipping a property becomes more common in markets that are rapidly appreciating in price.**

c) Almost all income producing real estate is put under a conditional contract to purchase prior to the actual closing. The buyer and seller agree in writing to a purchase and sale conditioned on the buyer having a certain period of time to conduct due diligence prior to the transfer of title. The price is fixed at the time the contract is signed. In an up market and during longer due diligence periods, the property may appreciate to a level that is above the contract price. Some buyers may become tempted to sell their contract to purchase to a third-party buyer at a profit. This is known as flipping. Flipping is also possible in situations where the seller ineffectively markets a property or naively agrees to sell it at a below market price.

Unsolicited Offers

62

a) Unsolicited offers are typical in almost all markets but particularly in markets that are rapidly accelerating in price. In high appreciation markets where buyers far outnumber sellers, it is typical that many buyers will directly solicit sellers and make offers. The goal is to avoid participating in bidding competitions that put greater upward pressure on prices.

b) A seller who accepts an unsolicited offer hoping that the prospective buyer is making a retail offering is a buyer's dream that typically turns out to be a seller's nightmare.

63 Due Diligence Checklist for Apartments

Due Diligence (DD) Checklist

LETTER OF INTENT

☐ Reviewed and Signed Off By _____
☐ Reviewed and Signed Off By Legal
☐ DD can expire without obligation by Buyer
☐ Deposit release requires affirmative written action
☐ Sufficient time for DD
☐ Sufficient time for Financing
☐ Deposit Goes Hard on _____

PURCHASE AGREEMENT

☐ Reviewed and Signed Off By _____
☐ Reviewed and Signed Off By Legal
☐ DD can expire without obligation by Buyer
☐ Deposit release requires affirmative written action
☐ Sufficient time for DD
☐ Sufficient time for Financing
☐ Deposit goes hard on_____
☐ Confirmed Investment Committee Date

Due Diligence (DD) Checklist

FINANCING
DEBT
- [ ] Lenders Selected
- [ ] Preliminary Numbers Sent To Lender(s)
- [ ] Lender Calendar of Dates Agreed To
- [ ] Lender Package Prepared/Sent
- [ ] All Lender Requir'd documents (rent rolls, etc) sent.
- [ ] Closing/Funding Date Agreed To
- [ ] All Legal/Finance costs included in Deal Summary

THIRD PARTY EQUITY
- [ ] Equity Source Selected
- [ ] Prelim Numbers Sent To Equity Source(s)
- [ ] Equity Calendar of Dates Agreed To
- [ ] All Equity Source Requir'd docs (rent rolls, etc) sent
- [ ] Closing/Funding Date Agreed To

COMPARABLE PROPERTIES
RENT COMPS
- [ ] Economic Rent Comps Completed
- [ ] Analyst/Property Mgt/Portfolio Mgr toured rent comps/ units
- [ ] Econ Rents tie to Deal Sheet
- [ ] Numeric Check for Accuracy

SALES COMPS
- [ ] Economic Sale Comps Completed
- [ ] Analyst/Portfolio Manager and Port. Mgr have toured Sale comps/units
- [ ] Numeric Check for Accuracy

Due Diligence (DD) Checklist

RENTAL INCOME
OBTAINED MOST CURRENT RENT ROLL
- [ ] Rent Roll totals verified / run tape
- [ ] In-Place Rents tie to Deal Sheet Actual Rents
- [ ] Street Rents tie to Deal Sheet
- [ ] Rents reconcile to Operating Statements

LEASE AUDIT COMPLETED
- [ ] Leases tie to rent roll
- [ ] Deposits tie to rent roll
- [ ] Move-in/Lease Expiration Dates tie to Rent Roll
- [ ] No indications of resident disputes with Landlord (correspondence)
- [ ] No indication of material delinquencies
- [ ] No Sideletter/sweetheart agreements/concessions
- [ ] Adequate Resident qualification (3x income)
- [ ] Tie Cash Deposits to Collected Rents

RENT GROWTH FORECAST
- [ ] Supported by research
- [ ] Source of rent growth numbers
- [ ] Rent Growth Used in Proforma for each year

VACANCY
- [ ] Historic Vacancy (years 1,2,3)
- [ ] Proforma Vacancy

BAD DEBT
- [ ] Historic Bad Debt
- [ ] Bad Debt included in Cash Flows

MODELS
- [ ] Does Property Currently Have Model Units
- [ ] How Many
- [ ] Type

Due Diligence (DD) Checklist

OTHER INCOME
☐ Obtained/Created Sched. of Other Income from Seller
☐ Analyze Other Income for durability

  Do not annualize non-recurring items !!

  Do not annualize forfeited deposits !!

LAUNDRY CONTRACTS
☐ When do they expire
☐ Who are they with
☐ Last time renewed
☐ What are vendor/landlord splits

CABLE CONTRACTS
☐ When do they expire
☐ Who are they with
☐ Last time renewed
☐ What are vendor/landlord splits

RUBS
☐ Does property use RUBS
☐ Which Vendor/Serivce Company
☐ Level of Penteration (number of units)
☐ Proforma penetration (number of units)

LAUNDRY INCOME
☐ Examined Contracts/Cancellable
☐ Can you install W/D's in Units
☐ If so, reduce Laundry Income accordingly

OTHER SOURCES OF OTHER INCOME

☐ _____

Due Diligence (DD) Checklist

OPERATING EXPENSES

GENERAL

- ☐ Obtained Seller List and Copies of all Service Contracts
  - ☐ Reviewed Service Contracts Cancellable in 30 days
  - ☐ Any exceptions
- ☐ Obtained list/copies, insurance claims for past year
- ☐ Obtained Seller List of Pending Litigation
- ☐ Obtained Seller provided list, Govmt. notices/actions
  - ☐ Condemnation
  - ☐ Emminent Domain
  - ☐ Wetlands claims
  - ☐ Environmental issues
  - ☐ Legal compliance with ordinances

ADVERTISING COSTS

- ☐ Reviewed all advertising contracts
- ☐ All Cancellable in 30 days
- ☐ Is owner using Internet Advertising
- ☐ All advertising costs included in Proforma
  - ☐ New leasing brochure design/production costs
  - ☐ Resident Retention parties/promotions
  - ☐ Welcome baskets, etc

TOTAL PAYROLL COSTS

- ☐ Number of Office Personnel
- ☐ Number of R&M Personnel
- ☐ Reviewed Historical Salaries/Total Comp
  - ☐ Bonuses/Leasing Incentives/Apartment Credits
- ☐ Proforma minimum of 1 person/50 units
  - ☐ Temp Personnel Costs included
  - ☐ Temp takeover costs included in Capital Budget

Due Diligence (DD) Checklist

☐ Workman's Comp In Proforma
☐ Updated Group Insurance in Proforma
☐ Leasing Bonuses, etc., in Proforma

GENERAL & ADMINISTRATION COSTS

☐ Office Leases
☐ Equipment Leases reviewed
☐ All Leases cancellable in 30 days
☐ Office Furniture lease reviewed
☐ Cancellable in 30 days
☐ Mailing Costs (FEDEX, Postage, etc.)
☐ Refreshments/Snacks
☐ Telephone Expense
☐ Sufficient lines in proforma for Internet as well
☐ Supplies
☐ Legal (Evictions. Pay or quits, etc.)
☐ Business Permits
☐ Pool Permits
☐ Janitorial

MANAGEMENT FEE COSTS

☐ Property Management Company selected
☐ Fee Agreed to/Included in Proforma
☐ Incentive fee agreed to/included in Proforma
☐ Mgmt. Co. has developed a Property Proforma
☐ Reviewed, Compared Mgmt. Co budget to Proforama
☐ Identified and Reconciled differences
☐ Adjusted Management Fee at Sale as follows:
☐ Deals under $8mm - 4%
☐ Deals over $8mm - 3%
☐ Pest Control Costs
☐ Reviewed Historicals for expense
☐ Unusual items or indication of recurring items
☐ Included in Proforma

Due Diligence (DD) Checklist

LANDSCAPE COSTS
- ☐ Reviewed Historical costs
- ☐ Unusual items
- ☐ General Condition of Existing Landscape
- ☐ Condition of irrigation system/clocks
- ☐ Obtained quote for Landscape Service
- ☐ Seasonal Color expense included in Proforma
- ☐ Landscape improvements fully budgeted for in Capital

SECURITY COSTS
- ☐ Reviewed Historical Security Costs
- ☐ Reviewed Crime Report for area
- ☐ Spoke w/ Police Dept. re: incidents at property
- ☐ Included appropriate security costs in the proforma
  - ☐ Install Gate
  - ☐ Drive-by Security
  - ☐ Resident Patrol

APARTMENT TURNOVER COSTS
- ☐ Reviewed Historical Turnover Rate
- ☐ Reviewed Historical Turnover Costs /Per Unit
- ☐ Applied Turnover Rate
- ☐ Applied turnover Costs Per Unit
- ☐ Unusual turnover expenditures [Wallpaper, stoves, etc]
  - ☐ Need levelors/verticals in /budgeted for

REPAIR & MAINTENANCE COSTS
- ☐ Reviewed Historical Maintenance Costs
  - ☐ Noted any unusual items
  - ☐ Pulled out non-recurring/capitalized items
  - ☐ Examined R&M Work Order Logs
  - ☐ Identified any unusual items
  - ☐ Properly budgeted in Proforma

Due Diligence (DD) Checklist

UTILITIES

☐ Examined Historical costs
☐ Service Providers :
☐   Water/Sewer
☐   Gas
☐   Electricity
☐   Trash
☐   Other
☐ Spoke with Utility providers re: forecast rate increases
☐   Included in proforma
☐ Evaluated possibility of RUBS
☐ Can property be separately metered

PROPERTY TAXES

☐ Obtained copies of tax bills for two prior years
☐ Contacted Assessor re: millage rates during hold period
☐ Applied full millage rate to purchase price for Proforma
☐ Determined existence of Special Assessments
☐   Included in Proforma as appropriate
☐ Adjusted Property Taxes as Sale to Full Sale Price

PROPERTY INSURANCE

☐ Obtained Insurance bid
☐   Proper allocation to insured improvements
☐   Included in proforma
☐ Personal Property Insurance quote obtained
☐ Earthquake Insurance necessary
☐   Obtained quote/included in proforma

Due Diligence (DD) Checklist

RESERVES
- ☐ Reviewed Historical Capital Expenditures
- ☐ Identified recurrring items of concern
- ☐ Developed appropriate reserve amounts
- ☐   Amount per unit per year
- ☐ Reserves at Sale adequate

TITLE ISSUES
- ☐ Title Company Selected
- ☐ Preliminary Title Received
- ☐ Title Exceptions Received
- ☐ Reviewed Title and Exceptions
- ☐ Seller provided pre-existing survey
- ☐ CC&R's Received
- ☐ Association dues in proforma
- ☐   Reviewed for onerous obligations/covenants
- ☐   Who pays title Buyer/Seller, split
- ☐ Title Costs Properly Quoted/Included in Financials
- ☐   Transfer Taxes for County AND City
- ☐   Transfer Taxes at TIME OF SALE TO THIRD PARTY
- ☐   Documentary Costs
- ☐   Escrow Fees
- ☐ Agreed all Proforma Closing Costs to Purch. Agreement
- ☐   Who pays escrow Buyer/Seller, split
- ☐ Survey Ordered for ALTA
- ☐   Plotted Encroachments
- ☐   Encroachment Endorsements Received
- ☐ Zoning Letter Ordered Received Date
- ☐ Parking Compliance Verified
- ☐ Zoning Compliance Verified
- ☐ Other

Due Diligence (DD) Checklist

THIRD PARTY DUE DILIGENCE

- ☐ Physical Inspections
- ☐ Internal Physical Inspections Completed
  - ☐ Unit Inspections
  - ☐ Electrical Wiring Inspections/Determination
  - ☐ Plumbing Inspections/Determination/Galvanized
  - ☐ Balconies/Decks System Condition
    (Cantilevered or Post)
  - ☐ Stairwell Condition
  - ☐ Roof Condition /Roofs Walked
  - ☐ Landscape Condition
  - ☐ Asphalt Condition
  - ☐ Lighting/ Security/Entrance/Carport, etc.
  - ☐ Retaining Wall Condition
  - ☐ Exterior Paint Condition
  - ☐ Pool Deck Condition
  - ☐ Pool Mechanicals Condition
- ☐ Reviewed/Examined Historical Capital Expenditures
  - ☐ Unusual Items
  - ☐ Recurring expenditures
- ☐ Obtained Copies of Certificates of Occupancy
- ☐ Obtained Copies of Operating/Pool Permits
- ☐ Examined Repair & Maintenance Logs for Recurring Items
  - ☐ Recurring roof leaks
  - ☐ Recurring plumbing issues, etc
- ☐ Completed all Deferred Maint/Capital Exp. Estimates
  - ☐ Estimates included in Proforma
  - ☐ Estimates reconciled/agree to third party reports
- ☐ Evaluated Washer/Dryer potential
- ☐ Evaluated Garage potential
- ☐ Determined Compliance with City Ordinances

Due Diligence (DD) Checklist

☐   Fire Code/Sprinklers
☐   Asbestos Abatement
☐ Determined Compliance with ADA
☐ Third Party Physical Firm Selected /Who
☐   FNMA Compliant
☐   Engagement Letter Executed by BOTH parties
☐   No Fatal Flaws
☐ Third Party Environmental Firm Selected
☐   FNMA Compliant
☐   Engagement Letter Executed by BOTH parties
☐   No Fatal Flaws
☐   Final Report Reviewed/Accepted
☐ Third Party Termite Company Selected
☐   Engagement Letter Executed by BOTH parties
☐   No Fatal Flaws
☐   Final Report Reviewed/Accepted
☐ Third Party Appraisal Firm Selected
☐   FNMA Compliant
☐   Engagement Letter Executed by BOTH parties
☐   Initial Value Received/Reviewed
☐   Final Report Reviewed/Accepted
☐ Third Party Property Tax Firm Selected /Who
☐   Engagement Letter Executed by BOTH parties
☐   Tax Estimates Received/Reviewed/Approved
☐   Final Report Reviewed/Accepted
☐ All Property Photos on computer

Due Diligence (DD) Checklist

FINAL APPROVAL CHECKLIST

- [ ] CEO has Toured Property
- [ ] Exec Summary ties to Deal Summary Numbers
- [ ] All numbers tie to detail Deal Summary/Net Proceeds
- [ ] Financial Review by accounting/CFO
- [ ] Econ. Sales Comps Reviewed for Consistency/Accuracy
- [ ] Rent Comp Adjust Worksheets Reviewed for Accuracy
- [ ] Rent Growth assumptions supported/signed of by CEO
- [ ] Financial Assumptions Page Reviewed/Accurate
- [ ] Refinance scenario Reviewed Accurate
- [ ] Exit Property Tax Adjustment Reviewed/ Accurate
- [ ] Sales Costs accurate
- [ ] Seller paid Transfer Taxes, etc at Sale included
- [ ] Deferred Maintenance numbers accurate
- [ ] Repositioning Costs & Rehab costs verified
- [ ] Overhead allocation included in Repositioning Costs
- [ ] Management Fee: Used 3% at Exit
- [ ] Weighted Avg Equity Outstanding Period
        Recalculated/Verified
- [ ] IRRS reviewed/verified
- [ ] Simple annual return reviewed/verified

CLOSING DETAILS

- [ ] Preliminary Settlement Statement Received
- [ ] Closing Rent Roll Received/Reviewed
- [ ] Prorations reviewed/Agreed to
- [ ] Tax calculation
- [ ] Rents
- [ ] Purchase Price on statement is correct
- [ ] Seller Credits on statement are correct

Due Diligence (DD) Checklist

- [ ] Payment of Closing Costs consistent with Contract
- [ ] Financing Amount is correct
  - [ ] Payment for points reviewed/approved
  - [ ] Other Finance costs reviewed/approved
  - [ ] Legal costs reviewed/approved
- [ ] Third Party Equity amount reviewed/Accurate
  - [ ] Third party equity related costs reviewed/accurate
- [ ] Total Cash Due from Buyer verified

Adjustments to Rents for Amenities

64

On the following page is a schedule of typical dollar adjustments to rents to account for amenity differences. As an example, if the subject property or property being acquired had enclosed garages for each unit and a competing project only had carport parking, other things being equal the subject property should have a $50 per unit premium ($75 for garages minus $25 for carports). An extensive local rental survey should precede assigning amenity values but the concept of relative values as shown should be a good baseline. Behind the relative values depicted there are surveys of thousands of units over a twenty year period.

PROJECT AMENITIES	ADJ. $/unit
Balcony / Patio	15
Carport Parking	25
Subterranean Parking	25
Enclosed Garages	75
Laundry Room	10
Swimming Pool/Spa	10
Sauna	5
Exercise Room	10
Secured Building & Perimeter	50
Community Room	10
Theater	5
Business Center	5
Sport Courts	5
UNIT AMENITIES	**ADJ. $**
Washer Dryer Connections in Unit	40
Washer Dryer Included in Unit	75
Air Conditioning Wall Unit	20
Central Air Conditioning	35
Mirrored Wardrobes/Walkin Closets	10
Dishwasher	10
Disposal	3
Refrigerator	30
Cable TV Available	0
Cable TV Paid	30
Utilities Paid	30
Fireplace	10
TOT. AMENITY ADJUSTMENT	

Principal Factors 65
Influencing Changes in
Real Estate Prices

The relative changes in the prices of investment real estate are most influenced by:

a) **Marcel Arsenault:** "The key is not projecting the problems of the past, but looking at the future and how cash flow could be increased."

b) **Ben Leeds:** "Real estate trades on future assumptions of income growth or contraction. Your ability to anticipate future cash flow should dramatically influence the financial structuring you do today."

c) **Anticipated increases or decreases in cash flow have the greatest short-term (six to twenty-four month) impact on the valuation of investment real estate.** Cash flow can be increased or decreased through changes in revenue, changes in expenses relative to revenue, and changes in the cost of debt or equity capital.

d) **The balance between the numbers of qualified buyers compared to the number of properties for sale has the second greatest short term influence** on the relative price changes of investment property. It should be noted that

an anticipated increase in cash flow usually results in more buyers entering the market.

e) In the longer term, the relative value of investment real estate is impacted more significantly by the changes in the yields of
competing investment opportunities.

**Recommended Reading
Internet Sites
Trade Organizations**

GENERAL REAL ESTATE TOPICS

National Commercial Property
For Sale/Lease
Database/Online
- Loopnet   loopnet.com
- CoStar   costar.com

National/Magazine/Online/News
- Commercial Property News   cpnonline.com
- National Real Estate Investor   nreionline.com
- Real Estate Forum   reforum.com
- Nat'l Mortgage News   nationalmortgagenews.com
- Real Estate Journal   realestatejournal.com

National/Research/Database/News
- National Real Estate Index   realestateindex.com
- REIS Reports   reis.com
- CoStar   costar.com
- Property & Portfolio Research   ppr.info/
- Real Capital Analytics   rcanalytics.com
- Bureau of Labor Statistics   bls.gov
- Economy.com   economy.com
- Bureau of the Census   census.gov
- Bureau of Economic Analysis   bea.doc.gov

National/Online/News/Information
- Inman News   inman.com
- PikeNet   pikenet.com
- Globe.St.com   globest.com

National/Newsletter/Online/News
- Robert Bruss R.E. Newsletter   bobbruss.com
- Crittenden Online   crittendenonline.com
- American City Business Journals   bizjournals.com

National/Tradeshow
- Realcomm   realcomm.com
- Inman Real Estate Connect   inman.com
- Real Share   realshareconferences.com

VARIOUS PROPERTY TYPES
National Trade Organizations
- Urban Land Institute   uli.org
- National Association of Real Estate Investment Trusts
  nareit.com

MULTIFAMILY
National/Magazine/Online
- Multifamily Executive   multifamilyexecutive.com
- Multi-Housing News   multi-housingnews.com

National Trade Organization
- National Apartment Association   naahq.org
- National Multi Housing Council   nmhc.org
- Urban Land Institute Multi-Family Council   uli.org
- Institute of Real Estate Management   irem.org

HOSPITALITY & LODGING
National/Magazine/Online
- Hotel Journal   hoteljournal.com
- Hospitality Food & Beverage Executive Magazine
  hfbexecutive.com
- Lodging Magazine   lodgingmagazine.com
- National Hotel Executive   hotelexecutive.com
- Hospitality Expos   hospitalityexpos.com

National Research
- Cornell Hospitality Research Center   hotelschool.
  cornell.edu

National Trade Organizations
- Urban Land Institute Hotel Development Council
  uli.org

RETAIL
National/Magazine/Online
- Globe Street Retail   globest.com/retail
- Retail Traffic   retailtrafficmag.com
- Shopping Center Business
  shoppingcenterbusiness.com

National Trade Organizations
- International Council of Shopping Centers   icsc.org
- Urban Land Institute Commercial & Retail Council
  uli.org
- Institute of Real Estate Management   irem.org

National Research
- Retail Tenants   retailtenants.com
- Market Insite Group   marketinsitegroup.com
- ESRI Business Information Solutions   esribis.com

OFFICE AND INDUSTRIAL
National/Magazine/Online
- Office & Industrial Props   officeandindustrial.com

National Trade Organizations
- Building Owners and Managers Association
- National Assoc of Indus and Office Prop   naiop.org
- Urban Land Inst. Office Develp. Council   uli.org
- Urban Land Inst. Indus. & Office Park
                    Development Council   uli.org
- Institute of Real Estate Management   irem.org

Index